Praise for *America's Best Colleges for B Students*

"This book contains practical information for any student searching for the right college 'fit' instead of simply trying to 'fit in' at the wrong college. From this small college's perspective, the 'solid B' student has the same chance as an A student to be successful in an environment where each is encouraged to develop his/her potential."

—Sandy Speed
Dean of Admission and Financial Aid
Schreiner University

"This book offers practical information and advice for students and parents alike. There is a great school out there for you—*America's Best Colleges for B Students* will help you find it!"
—Mark Campbell
Vice-President for Enrollment Management
McKendree College

"At last, a college resource book for real students and real families. We hear so much about how only over achievers get into good schools that we forget that college isn't just about grades and tests scores; it's about learning, living and moving forward. This is something that all students need, regardless of their high school performance. Tamra Orr has given families the tools to help their young adults find the perfect college for them. An invaluable resource!"

—Teri Brown
Author of *Day Tripping: Your Guide to Educational Family Adventures*

"Tamra Orr's refreshingly candid approach to the college search dispels the fear that B students and their families often face. An easy yet information-packed read!"

—Bethany Bierman
Assistant Director Office of Undergraduate Admissions
Augsburg College

"Many hard-working kids (this book calls them B students) don't think they're college material because they don't have high college boards or the highest grades. In short order, this book dispels that myth! Tamra Orr has gathered helpful insights and suggestions that will, thankfully, elevate the expectations of such students to achieve college success."

—Patrick J. O'Brien
Retired high school counselor, former Marquette Northern California admissions representative and current ACT ambassador

"This excellent 'advice' book is a must read for those students and their parents who want to understand and navigate the process and find the right match toward that important degree."

—Karen P. Condeni
Vice President and Dean of Enrollment
Ohio Northern University

"This book will be a terrific introduction to the college search process. The format offers helpful suggestions in a non-intimidating approach. For many high school students the college process becomes a seemingly insurmountable task. *America's Best Colleges for B Students* is a terrific introductory tool that outlines the basic steps to begin the college search process."

—Amanda (Mandy) Warhurst Webster
Senior Associate Director of Admission
Salve Regina University

"Tamra Orr's book is just what the 'not so perfect' student needs. The advice is to the point and incredibly useful. You don't have to attend a huge Ivy League school to get a superior education. Orr's book should be required reading for individuals of all ages who are thinking of attending college."

—Sandra Roy
Educator and author

"What really makes a great student great? Is greatness limited to a letter grade on paper or a score on the SATs? There is so much more that factors into it like the sincere desire to not only succeed in the classroom, but succeed in life. There are some outstanding institutions of higher learning that understand that reality and offer programs from which B students will benefit the most as well as learning services that help them become better students. By offering an in-depth analysis of the best schools catering to the needs of real world students, this book will go far in helping families identify the best schools that suit individual needs. Education is not 'one size fits all,' and this book helps explain that—and will help anyone in search of higher education find the 'right fit.'"

—Jennifer A. Fiorentino
Director, Public Relations & Communications
Dean College

"With humor and insight, Tamra Orr sets the record straight about college admission, offering practical advice and hope to college-bound students. This book makes the important point that the college admission process doesn't need to be fraught with stress and anxiety. Many bright, interesting teens that underperformed in high school will recognize themselves in the pages of this book. Orr guides students in how to explore colleges where they can find themselves and achieve as never before."

—Joan Casey
College Planning Consultant
Educational Advocates, Brookline, Mass.

"Finally! A guide for motivated late bloomers—solid students who in the right environment will flourish. Tamra Orr has done her homework to provide you with the guidance and tips you need to find the college that's right for you—and help you succeed once you're there. Pack your suitcase for adventure and bring your drive, energy and personal commitment to achieve!"

—Esther Goodcuff
Associate Vice President for Enrollment Management and Student Affairs
Adelphi University

America's Best Colleges for B Students

A College Guide for Students without Straight A's

By Tamra B. Orr

America's Best Colleges for B Students: A College Guide for Students without Straight A's

By Tamra B. Orr

Published by SuperCollege, LLC
4546 B10 El Camino Real, #281
Los Altos, CA 94022
www.supercollege.com

Credits: Cover design TLC Graphics, www.TLCGraphics.com. Design: Monica Thomas.

Trademarks: All brand names, product names and services used in this book are trademarks, registered trademarks or tradenames of their respective holders. SuperCollege is not associated with any college, university, product or vendor.

Disclaimers: The author and publisher have used their best efforts in preparing this book. It is intended to provide helpful and informative material on the subject matter. Some narratives and names have been modified for illustrative purposes. SuperCollege and the author make no representations or warranties with respect to the accuracy or completeness of the contents of the book and specifically disclaim any implied warranties or merchantability or fitness for a particular purpose. There are no warranties which extend beyond the descriptions contained in this paragraph. The accuracy and completeness of the information provided herein and the opinions stated herein are not guaranteed or warranted to produce any particular results. SuperCollege and the author specifically disclaim any responsibility for any liability, loss or risk, personal or otherwise, which is incurred as a consequence, directly or indirectly, of the use and application of any of the contents of this book.

ISBN: 1932662065

Manufactured in the United States of America

10 9 8 7 6 5 4 3 2 1

Cataloging-in-Publication Data
Tamra B. Orr
    America's Best Colleges for B Students: A College Guide for Students without Straight A's
        p.   cm.
    Includes appendices and index.
    ISBN 1932662065
    1. College Admission   I. Title
    2. Reference   3. Education

*To my kids who brighten my life, my husband who enriches my life
and my parents who gave me life.*

Table of Contents

Foreword

If the prospect of receiving an A- in AP calculus keeps you up at night, this book is not for you. If, on the other hand, you are ecstatic about scoring that B in English, this book is exactly for you!

One of the greatest myths about a college education is that you need to have straight A's or be the class valedictorian to get into an excellent college. The truth is that there are terrific colleges out there that want you—whether you are a B student or, gasp, even a C student. But don't assume that these colleges are looking for slackers. Quite the opposite: These schools know that good students don't always perform at their true potential in high school. For example:

- Maybe you didn't take high school seriously and only now have come to realize the importance of doing well academically.

- Maybe you managed your time poorly or were overcommitted with a job or activities.

- Maybe you were distracted by events in your life beyond your control.

- Maybe you were just bored with high school.

Whatever the reason, these schools know that your grades and test scores are not always reflective of who you are and how well you will do in college. So, if you are now committed to getting a college education and are willing to put in the time and effort to be a successful student, these colleges want you.

The key is: How do you find these colleges? What do you need to look for to make sure that you will excel? And how do you show the college that you are serious about getting a great education and will be an asset to their student body?

That's where this book will help. Here are just a few of the things that you will learn:

- How to identify colleges that accept students with less than perfect grades and test scores.

- What characteristics to look for in a college to ensure that you succeed academically as well as socially.

■ How to best position yourself—both the positives and negatives—in the college application, essay and interview.

■ Ways to pay for your education. (Scholarships are not just reserved for the A students. There are literally thousands also available for students based on non-academic skills and talents.)

■ Tips for making that sometimes difficult transition from high school to college.

Tamra Orr has written this book just for you. She has been there, done that as a student like you without perfect grades or test scores. She knows there is no shame in being a B student. (In fact, Tamra knows how to present this as a huge positive to a college!) She also knows that just because you may not be in the "Ivy-League-Wannabe" Crowd doesn't mean you are not motivated and committed to being successful.

Let her help you find that perfect college! We wish you the best in your journey!

—Gen and Kelly Tanabe
Authors of nine books on college planning including *Get into Any College* and *Sallie Mae How to Pay for College*

Introduction

Once upon a time, long, long ago, almost anyone who could find a way to afford going to college (and had a high school diploma or GED) went to college. SAT just meant the past tense of "sit" and GPA was an odd combination of letters that might have been a neat abbreviation for "Grandpa." After World War II, tests and test scores started to gain in importance, but it would be some time before they would become the determining factor behind going to college. Sure, if you had a great SAT score or a really high GPA it was easier to get scholarships or get the really BIG colleges to give you more than a glance. But I remember applying to colleges without much thought at all about my numbers (dating myself, that was back in the late 1970s). I was too busy scoping out the campus, checking the ratio of guys to girls and, oh yeah, seeing what majors were offered. (Although 30 years later, I can STILL tell you my SAT scores.)

The picture is quite different today. Getting into college is not only more expensive, but also much tougher. Colleges are getting more selective to the point that even valedictorians with a 4.0 average and perfect SAT scores are being turned away from some of the Ivy League institutions.

Because of this, many students are ready to throw their hands up in the air and say, "Ok, I get it! I don't have good enough numbers, so I obviously can't go to college. I'll just forget it!" If you are among them, realize this: You, yes YOU, are the reason for this book. It is designed to do two things: help you realize what it takes to get into many colleges (and an overview of what happens after you do) and which ones are eagerly awaiting your application.

For starters, get rid of the myths/assumptions you might have about choosing a college. If you believe any of the following, take them from the "The Earth is Round" list (truth) and put them in the "Santa Claus/ Tooth Fairy" list (fantasies). Here we go:

- You need a perfect GPA or SAT to get into a good college.

- The best way to pick a college is rankings in a magazine article/your best friend's recommendation/the names you recognize the most.

- Traditional four-year colleges are the only ones employers will accept.

- Only the large colleges are worth attending.

- Your college should have more students than your high school does.

- Small colleges offer inferior classes, faculty and degrees.

None of these statements is true.

- A perfect score or transcript is not required at most colleges, as you will see as you read this book.

- The best way to select a college is not to take someone else's word for it but to do your homework (yes, MORE homework) and find out which colleges best suit you and your preferences.

- While four-year colleges are the norm, there are many two-year programs and other options that are just as appealing to future employers.

- Small colleges often offer the conditions and student/teacher ratio that will ensure a high-quality, successful education. In no way are their classes, faculty or degrees inferior to those of the larger universities.

One of the biggest myths of all about college, of course, is that even if you find one that you like and will accept you, you will not be able to afford it. We will dispel that myth as well in Chapter Six.

You, standing right there in the middle of the library or bookstore (or at home scanning the intro because your parents told you to "READ THIS!"), you with the 2.9 or 3.1 GPA or the 1560 new SAT score or 19 composite ACT cannot only go to a college or university, but you can also go to a wonderful institution where you will make friends, have fun, grow up and yeah, learn a lot of stuff and get a degree. These colleges are not runners-up to the "good" places; they are wonderful schools that are willing to look beyond the numbers to the person standing behind them. They have admission departments that give your scores some thought, and then put them down and search for the human being on the other side of the digits. And really, isn't that what you would want them to do anyway? You are certainly more than any group of numbers could possibly represent.

This book was written to guide you to lots of helpful information about 100 colleges and universities that want you to be a part of their student population. It will also show you how to:

- Make the best out of the time you still have left in high school

- Make a great impression on the college admission department through both the essay and interview

- Explain those less-than-stellar numbers and let your strengths shine through

- Survive in college once you get there

Belonging is one of the strongest natural drives inside each and every person. You want to find a college where you are happy, comfortable, accepted and belong. They want students who feel like they have found a new home. Let this book be your guide to that relationship.

CHOOSING

How to Choose the Right College for You

CHAPTER ONE
• • • • • • • • •

Where to Find Colleges That Welcome B Students

We Really Do Want You (Or, Why Colleges Love B Students...)

There are more than 3,400 four-year, accredited colleges and universities in this country. That's a lot of places to learn! You can be sure that there are many schools for everyone and there certainly are many choices for B students. Your statistics may make the search a little longer and a bit challenging, but no less rewarding.

Nothing is as important to your educational success as finding a college where you feel comfortable. A key to success is being flexible and prepared to give the avenues open to you a fair chance. You have to be willing to look a little deeper and explore options, some of which you may not have thought of before. For instance, "Keep an open mind about going out of state," encourages Lynda McGee, college counselor at Downtown Magnets High School in downtown Los Angeles. It is McGee's personal goal to find schools for all students. "Some students fear leaving the area, especially those in sunny California," she explains.

Judi Robinovitz, an educational consultant for more than 25 years, suggests that students be open to exploring colleges they may not already know about. "You have to dispel the notion that just because you have not heard of a college, it's a bad college," she says.

"There are no bad colleges," exclaims Patrick O'Brien, former admission officer and consultant-ambassador for the ACT. "Remember, the 'best' school is the one that is best for you, not necessarily the ones that are highlighted in the books," says O'Brien.

But, why would a college be willing to take a chance on a student that doesn't have the kind of scores and grades they usually require?

It's simple: They have common sense.

First, a number of universities want a diverse student body roaming around their campuses. To achieve this, they have to broaden their ideas of what kind of student they will accept. Just as colleges accept people from all kinds of financial, ethnic, religious and racial backgrounds, they often will accept those with various levels of academic achievement. This is the key to diversity.

Second, admission officers often realize that while students may not have the most perfect numbers, they can still add greatly to the student body. They may be tremendous leaders, facilitators, speakers or organizers. They may exhibit strength in a variety of skills that can't be pinpointed with the average test scores. While they may not perform well in math, they may excel in the humanities. They may enrich the campus community in untold ways.

Last, colleges know that some students are genuinely working toward starting over, to changing their priorities and standards. Often this can be seen in school transcripts. Grades are improving with time; a new leaf has been turned over. Colleges recognize that some students really do go through difficult times such as the severe illness or death of a family member. Because of this, they are frequently willing to overlook some weak numbers and support that new dedication by accepting you into their college and giving you another way to continue that new trend.

So the college that you assumed was out of reach because of your grades or test scores, may actually be entirely possible if you can give them a reason for why you deserve to be there.

Looking Outside the Box

One secret to finding the right college is to look beyond the most popular schools that everyone in your area is applying to and to think outside of the box. Before you start shaking your head because they aren't what you had in mind, at least do a little research. Look at their site online, and check out the profiles at the end of this book. You can't say you don't like a place until you have enough information to know (otherwise known as innocent until proven guilty!)

Some schools that may be more open to B students include:

- career-oriented colleges

- community colleges

- all men's colleges

- all women's colleges

- very small colleges

"Community colleges are stepping stones to four-year universities, and they cost less, build skills and develop maturity. Students in the community college system gradually get into the college culture but with the security of home and familiar circumstances."

—Patrick O'Brien, former admission officer and consultant-ambassador for the ACT

Don't Overlook Community College

For many students, one of the best options remains the local community college. Yeah, you still have to live in your hometown, and most likely, still at home with your family, but you benefit from a good education while saving some big bucks for the future or for transferring to a four-year college. Community colleges are also much more open to students with B or C averages than some four-year institutions, so they can be a great solution for you.

But hey, you've heard some rumors about community colleges, right? You've heard them called everything from "Only Chance College" to "Harvard on the Highway." Like everything else, community colleges have a few myths surrounding them, and—here's a real surprise—most of them just aren't true. For instance:

- A degree from a community college is not as good as a university degree.

That just doesn't make any sense. An apple is an apple. A degree is a degree. You did the work and earned the diploma. Is it the same thing as a degree from Harvard? Ok, maybe not, but most of the time it will still get you through the front door and into the job.

- *The people who go to community college couldn't get in anywhere else.*

Not true. They go to community college because it's convenient, less expensive, allows them to keep working, gives them a chance to save money, provides a quality education and sometimes serves as a stepping ground to a traditional college.

■ *The faculty at community colleges is inferior to that at four-year institutions.*

The faculties and staff at community colleges and other colleges are quite comparable. They both have their degrees and years of experience to share with you.

■ *The credits from a community college will not transfer to other colleges.*

They certainly do.

■ *Since community colleges cost so much less, they can't be any good.*

They are just as good but do not have the incredible overhead a residential college has.

In 2004, the American Association of Community Colleges conducted a survey to see what the hottest programs at these colleges were. The survey found that the top five fields to study were allied health (46.6 percent), skilled trades/industrial, public services, information technologies and business.

Community College Facts

Here are some of the current stats on community colleges, thanks to the helpful people at the American Association of Community Colleges (www.aacc.nche.edu):

Public institutions	979
Private institutions	148
Tribal institutions	30
TOTAL	1,157

11.6 million students currently enrolled
6.6 million for credit and 5 million for non-credit

46% of all U.S. undergraduates
45% of first-time freshmen
58% women; 42% men
62% part time; 38% full time
47% of African-American undergrads
56% of Hispanic undergrads
48% of Asian/Pacific Islander undergrads
57% of Native American undergrads

Average tuition and fees: $2,076, and 37.8% of students receive some kind of financial aid.
More than 490,000 associate degrees
Almost 235,000 two-year certificates

Go, Team, Go!

Remember that choosing a college is not usually an individual choice. Instead, it takes a team of people all working together, including your teachers, advisers, guidance counselors, principals, coaches and family members. You need help with a decision this big, because it is a complex one.

There are so many colleges that accept B students that it is important for you to consider many different elements when you start your search. Ask yourself these questions:

- What kind of student am I now and what do I want to be in the future?

- What part of school do I like the best and least now?

- What does the idea of success actually mean to me?

- Where do I see myself in two years? Five years? 10 years?

- What part of the country appeals most to me?

- Do I want a small, intimate college or a bustling, exciting university?

- What percentage of males and females would be ideal for me?

- What is the cost and how much financial aid does each school offer?

- What are the most popular majors and is mine in that list?

- Do I want to be involved in a sorority/fraternity?

- Will I have any scholarships or grants that affect where I can go?

- Do I want a philosophical or religious college?

You may not know the answers to all these questions yet. Many of them will only come after you have taken some tours, read your research and talked to your team. Giving them some thought now, however, will give you a head start.

What to Look for in a College

The colleges profiled in this book do more than just accept B students. They are dedicated to helping them. They may offer a first-year general studies, remedial or transition class to help get you started. Many offer on-campus writing clinics and tutoring services. When you get in touch with the reps from these colleges, be prepared to ask them what services they might offer. Can you record lectures? Are there faculty advisers for each student? Are classes offered to help with the transition to college? Even if they don't have any plans in place (which is unlikely) your request might just be enough to implement one.

Let's take an up-close look at each of these options for a moment. It's important for you to think about which of these features are important to you and will help you succeed in college. Take notes so that when you contact a college rep or admission officer, you can ask if these choices exist at the school:

TUTORING: A variety of types of tutoring is available on virtually every campus. The only question is what format you prefer. You can check into peer tutoring, from either a classmate or friend; faculty tutoring from a willing professor; in-depth tutoring from a teacher's assistant or special on-campus centers and clinics. While some tutors may charge a fee, most services tend to be free. When you speak with a college rep, ask what might be available if you should need extra assistance.

COUNSELING: While tutoring is helpful with understanding a certain assignment or class subject, counseling is a wider scope. A counselor will help you make bigger decisions like what major to choose, what classes to take and what directions to go in. An academic counselor will not only help you reach academic goals, but also will quite often help you with emotional and mental stresses. To do your best academically, you need to be in good shape mentally. Counselors can recommend resources, give suggestions and tips, connect you with helpful mentors or organizations and much more.

CLASS SIZE AND PROFESSOR/STUDENT RATIO: One of the biggest advantages of small colleges is small classes. While many universities, even the really large ones, state that their average class size is between 10 and 30, a number of small colleges have fewer students per class. Instead of 22:1 student to professor ratios, they may have 5:1. There are many positive things about small classes—but they also have their negative sides as well. For example, your professors are much more likely to be aware of you, so if you are struggling or having a problem, they will be more apt to recognize it and reach out. On the other hand, it also means that if you miss class, they know (in a class of several hundred, it is a lot less noticeable, believe me!). If your homework isn't turned in, it will be observed right away as well. Small classes mean you can ask more questions and discuss things deeper. It also frequently means that participation will play a role in your overall grade.

Last, small classes can make the transition from high school to college easier. You will not feel so much like a minnow floundering around in a huge ocean. You will get to know your fellow classmates much easier and quicker if there are a half dozen rather than hundreds. Smaller classes often create more of a sense of cooperation between students than competition. Instead of trying to do better than another person, you will only be trying to do better than you have done before—the best kind of competition there is.

One thing to note about the numbers you find for professor/student ratio. It's important to go beyond the statistics. Ask students who attend the school how much they interact with their professors and how much of an effort the professors make to

A College Whose Door Is Always Open

The core philosophy of the community college in America can be captured in the phrase "access and excellence." Community colleges, like all institutions of higher education, struggle to be excellent. But when it comes to "access," there is no struggle at all; community colleges are the access institutions of the 21st century.

The community college has emerged as the institution of the second chance—even the third and fourth chance. Community colleges take great pride in their "open-door philosophy," which means that any student who has graduated from high school or who has reached a certain age will be admitted. This philosophy and practice is remarkably different from those of most four-year colleges and universities. Historically, most four-year colleges and universities require that students meet certain criteria for admission, eliminating those who are under-prepared or unqualified to compete.

Community colleges are willing to give all applicants an opportunity to succeed regardless of their history. That does not mean that an unprepared student will be admitted into a very challenging program such as nursing or engineering technology. Instead, through assessment and advising, students who are not prepared for more challenging work will be guided into developmental education programs where they will receive special tutoring and courses in which they can develop the skills for more advanced work.

The focus of the community college—through its faculty and innovative programs and practices—is to help students succeed, regardless of their level of achievement when they enter.

—Terry O'Banion, former president of the League for Innovation in the Community College

help their students. More important than the ratio of professors to students is how involved the professors will be in your studies.

TEACHING STYLES: Another question to look into when choosing your college is what different teaching styles the school may offer. What emphasis does it have on lab time? Is there a period of internship? How much of class time is hands-on activities for kinesthetic learners? How much is written out for visual learners? How much can be taped for auditory learners? Are there a lot of field trips? All of these options can make learning easier for many students like you. They are alternatives to the typical lecture/listen teaching format that dominated your education up until now. Colleges offer new ways to learn and excel.

PASS/FAIL or CREDIT/NO CREDIT CLASSES: Not all colleges offer classes with pass/fail grading systems but a number of them have used it effectively, including: Millikin University, University of Iowa, University of Illinois, Ohio State University, Stanford University, Tufts, University of California (Berkeley), Syracuse University, Pennsylvania State University, Pomona College and Grinnell College.

There are certainly a number of perks to this type of grading system. It often encourages students to explore classes that they may otherwise have ignored. For example, if you are an English major, you may not be brave enough to take an advanced math class because you will be surrounded by students who excel in math and competing with them might be overwhelming. However, if you know that you are only going to have to achieve a pass grade, you may be willing to go for it. With pass/fail, there is often less pressure on you; conversely, you may mistakenly think that you don't have to try at all (then you are just wasting everyone's time!).

In addition to regular classes, some types of learning fit the pass/fail system better than the traditional A, B, C, D and F. This is especially true for laboratory experiments, hands-on activities, thesis work and research.

"Getting the right college is not a game to be won, but a match to be made."

—**David Miller, director of college counseling at Stevenson School, Pebble Beach, California**

Is there a downside to this type of grading system? Naturally. Some of these courses can't be counted toward your major. While taking a class that doesn't count toward your major may seem unwise, it can be a smart move. You might discover a new passion, interest or direction for your education. You might also find out that you are better at a subject than you had imagined. The classes might even lead you to deciding on a minor—or changing your major. It's simply an invitation to go down another new college pathway.

THE EMPHASIS ON FINAL EXAMS: Another option to explore is how much influence final exams have on your overall grades. If you are the type who suffers from test anxiety (more on that later) or just does not test well, you want to look for colleges that offer options to traditional testing. Maybe oral tests are possible. Maybe you can earn most of your grades through homework, in class participation and other activities.

SUPPORT NETWORK AND LEVEL OF COMPETITION: Besides the formal support network provided by the school from tutoring and counseling, find out more about the informal support network. Do students tend to help each other or compete against each other? At some schools, students frequently work together on group projects or have study sessions together. At other schools, students work more independently. This is especially important if you learn better in a group environment.

SPECIAL PROGRAMS: Investigate what kind of special programs the colleges may offer. For example, some colleges offer co-op programs in which you're able to spend a semester gaining hands-on work experience with a company while earning credits. Most schools have study abroad programs that allow you to study internationally, but they vary in their size and scope. Special programs like these may appeal to you and may be just what you need to get motivated.

POSSIBLE AND POPULAR MAJORS: As you look through colleges listed in this book, take special note of the majors listed in each one. These are the most popular ones at that particular school. Why is it important to choose a college that features your major? It is just like going shopping. If you really want a pair of boot-cut jeans, you aren't going to go to a shoe store. You want to go where the clerks know what you are talking about and can lead you directly to many choices that fit your needs, right? Same thing with a college. If you want to be in computer tech, a college that specializes in art may not be the best choice. You want the school that is familiar with your major and can offer a strong faculty and curriculum in your choice.

You also want to check with a college rep and ask if you can have a double major at their college (and not just CAN YOU, but will you get the support and guidance you need if you choose to) or can you create your own major. The more options you have, the better the chance of having a college education tailored to your unique needs and the stronger the possibility of overall success.

What if you are undecided about your major when you start your college search? Relax—you are far from being the only one. Make a list of the most likely areas you'd like to explore and then look to see which colleges offer them. It is a first step.

Where to Find Out More About Colleges

■ **College fairs.** Dozens or even hundreds of college representatives will come to your town for college fairs. This is your opportunity to ask questions and get a personal perspective from these colleges without leaving the city limits. Get a list of upcoming college fairs from your counselor or at www.nacac. com/fairs.html.

■ **College representatives at your school.** Be sure to attend these events! You may be tempted to spend the time doing something else, but these can give you the perfect opportunity to learn a lot about a school. You may also be meeting the people who will eventually review your application if you submit one to that school. If you make a good impression, your chances of admission may rise.

■ **College catalogs/view books.** These may vary from a simple, colorful tri-fold pamphlet to a 40-page catalog, complete with DVD and/or CD, business cards with contact names, testimonials from students and dozens of photographs. Read them through carefully because they can answer many of your most common questions.

■ **College websites.** Whether you look online at home, in the library or at school, take the time to look over the websites of some of the colleges you are interested in. They almost always have a FYI/FAQ section that will answer basic questions. You also get a chance to see what the campus looks like, what some students have to say about the place (all glowing, of course!) and much more.

■ **College alumni.** For great suggestions and insight into a college, see if you can get in touch with someone who actually attended it. It might be your cousin, your father's co-worker, someone your guidance counselor suggested or a person the college itself refers you to speak with. Make a list of questions for that person ahead of time so you are sure to cover what you most want to find out. If the person graduated more than a few years ago, some information might not be as current as you need, but you can still learn some important facts.

■ **College visits and tours.** While this topic will be discussed more later in this book, it is important to realize that nothing makes a place come alive as much as visiting it. You can read about a university in every possible source, but you can't really know it until you visit it. That's when you can personally taste the cafeteria creations, hear the conversations in the student union and see the layout of the dorms in some of the residence halls. Go on a tour with your class, counselor, friends or family. The information you will gather is invaluable.

■ **College online virtual tours.** While going to a college in person is the best option, it is not always possible for a variety of reasons. In that case, be sure to at least go to a college's website and check out their virtual tours. You can get a better idea of whether this is the kind of place that calls to you—or not.

■ **Guidance counselors.** These wonderful people can give you a lot of helpful information about individual colleges. They may have printed material, website suggestions, contact names and more. Just ask!

■ **The school or local community library.** While this book is a great source for finding out about schools that welcome B and C students, there are tons more books out there that list options. Check them out and look up the ones you are most interested in to find out information. Spend some time just browsing through them as well. You may encounter some that you have not heard of before but are intriguing possibilities.

Visit Colleges Sooner than Later

Don't wait a moment longer to go and visit schools. Seeing is believing! Reading about a place in a book or online is fine for background information, but it is a visit that will give you the true feel of the college's atmosphere, attitudes and activities. (To find out what college tours are like, check out the website www.campustours.com).

Patrick O'Brien, former admission officer and consultant-ambassador for the ACT, says, "The more opportunities to visit college campuses as a junior or in the first part of senior year, the better. And don't just go for the standard college tour of the campus and facilities. Check out the dorms and dorm life," he advises. "Insist on visiting a class in a field of interest—it will show you how the college academic system really works." Try not to visit colleges during summer, however. As O'Brien says, "Never visit a campus when school is not in session; that's like visiting your high school on a weekend—dullsville." Don't depend on mom, dad or your guidance counselor to contact the school for a tour either. Do it yourself; it shows that college that you have initiative.

When you go for a campus tour, take part of your college-finding team with you so you can get their impressions of each place too. Don't spend your time exploring the things you can get from the school's website. Pretend you are an anthropologist from the future and study the place like we study primitive cultures today. Watch the students interact, check out the food sources, find out how the place accepts those from different ethnic, political or religious backgrounds, gays or married couples. Read the posters in the buildings and the bulletin boards in dorms. What announcements do they have? What are some of the upcoming events and activities? Do they have a choir, band or orchestra? How about a drama group? Hang out in the student union and see what goes on there. Is there a lot of diversity on the campus? Go by the bookstore and see what souvenirs you like. Check out the shopping area around the campus. Pick up a campus newspaper to read later.

Remembering all of your impressions of the places you have seen will not be easy. After you have seen a couple of campuses, facts and opinions will begin to mesh and soon you will find yourself asking which college had that great library. Do you remember what campus had those huge trees and large, green lawns? To prevent this from happening, make up a form to write down your thoughts as you tour a place. You can give schools a score of 1 (horrible) to 10 (perfection itself), plus a spot for general comments, thoughts and questions to follow up on later.

On the opposite page is an example of the kind of form you could use. If you don't like it, my feelings aren't hurt. Create your own! Design it the way that fits best for you.

College Score Sheet

Name of school: _____

Date visited: _____

Who went with me: _____

Contacts I made at the school: _____

_____

FOOD   1 2 3 4 5 6 7 8 9 10

CAMPUS   1 2 3 4 5 6 7 8 9 10

DORMS   1 2 3 4 5 6 7 8 9 10

GREEK   1 2 3 4 5 6 7 8 9 10

COMMUNITY   1 2 3 4 5 6 7 8 9 10

_____   1 2 3 4 5 6 7 8 9 10

_____   1 2 3 4 5 6 7 8 9 10

TOTAL SCORE:_____

How does the place make me feel? _____

Best part about the place: _____
_____
_____

Worst part about the place: _____
_____
_____

What is the city like? _____
_____
_____

What special services are offered to help B students? _____
_____
_____

Overall comments _____
_____
_____
_____
_____

College Score Sheet

Name of school: _____

Date visited: _____

Who went with me: _____

Contacts I made at the school: _____
_____

FOOD   1   2   3   4   5   6   7   8   9   10

CAMPUS   1   2   3   4   5   6   7   8   9   10

DORMS   1   2   3   4   5   6   7   8   9   10

GREEK   1   2   3   4   5   6   7   8   9   10

COMMUNITY   1   2   3   4   5   6   7   8   9   10

_____   1   2   3   4   5   6   7   8   9   10

_____   1   2   3   4   5   6   7   8   9   10

TOTAL SCORE:_____

How does the place make me feel? _____

Best part about the place: _____
_____
_____

Worst part about the place: _____
_____
_____

What is the city like? _____
_____
_____

What special services are offered to help B students? _____
_____
_____

Overall comments _____
_____
_____
_____
_____

The Sky's the Limit

Once you start looking for colleges you'll be overwhelmed at how many great choices there are. In fact, your problem may be too many options!

After you have a list of colleges, the next step is to fill out the applications. This is your opportunity to make your case to the college for why you should be accepted. While most colleges do look at your numbers (GPA, SAT, ACT), they will also look to your character. They will want to know your aspirations, your passions, your level of responsibility and maturity and how you choose to spend your time. Who inspires you? Who influences you? What do you expect of yourself? College admission officers see countless numbers of applications, many with high numbers, but it is the student that shows integrity, curiosity, originality and independence that will catch their eyes. Unlike grading those little #2 pencil filled in dots on the standardized tests, this kind of information is much harder to measure. The college application will go a long way to help paint that very unique portrait.

But before we hit the application, let's look at some of the last minute things you can do now to make sure you maximize your time in high school and set yourself up to create the strongest application possible.

CHAPTER TWO

• • • • • • • • • •

It's Never Too Late: Make a Change for the Better Right Now

Procrastination (pro-kras-ten-a-shun): that annoying habit that tends to follow us throughout our lives, convincing us that we can easily put off until tomorrow what we should be doing today (or yesterday) and not have to pay any consequences. (For an example, see the character of Scarlett O'Hara in the classic *Gone with the Wind*, who coined the phrase, "Fiddle-dee-dee, I'll think about it tomorrow!")

We've all done it. You will start the project/diet/chore/book report/ whatever tomorrow. Tomorrow, as little red-headed Annie reminded everyone in a relatively annoying song, is always a day away. It's eternally full of promise and potential. Unfortunately, when tomorrow arrives, it's today already, so we just repeat the mantra and everything is bumped one more time.

When it comes to getting ready for college, procrastination can be positively lethal. You already know that multiple forms have to be turned in early, from application to financial aid requests. It doesn't stop there. If your grades and test scores are not where you want them to be, there are no overnight miracles, potions or cures you can use. But there are steps you can take to brighten the picture a bit, especially if you are still in your sophomore or junior year.

Here is the list. Read it now (don't wait until tomorrow and you will already have a leg up on the competition). Some of these things are fairly simple; others take a lot of self-discipline. Fortunately, that is good practice for your college days ahead.

(1) Reorganize your priority list.

At the risk of sounding like your parents (and one day, you will realize how intelligent they really are), one of the first steps is to make school a top priority. That does not mean never seeing your friends or giving up any semblance of a social life. Instead, it simply means that when you think about your day, school should be high up on the list, somewhere below breathing, eating and drinking but way above watching *The Three Stooges* marathon on television.

If you have homework and your best friend calls and asks you to come over and hang out, give it some thought. Do your best to look beyond the fun of the moment to the potential reward down the road. It's not easy—but it is a mature thing to do (so be sure and let your parents know you made the responsible decision and earn a few brownie points in the process).

By making school a priority, other things will fall into line. Doing homework and studying for tests mean better grades, and better grades mean a higher GPA and most likely a better performance on the SAT or ACT. In turn, both of those will strengthen your chances of getting into more colleges. Amanda (Mandy) Warhurst Webster, senior associate director of admission at Salve Regina University, says, "Students must realize that the senior year is very important. You have to remain focused on academics and come in with a very strong first semester."

(2) Use your summers wisely.

Counting down the days to summer break is an educational tradition. Imagining how you are going to spend those long, hot, lazy summer days can keep you occupied for hours. Chances are your plans include sleeping in, being with friends, finding a beach, exploring a career as a couch potato and generally doing as little as possible. Without ruling out those possibilities, why not include a few things that could actually raise your chance of college admission? Here are a few possibilities:

■ **Get a job that will teach you important skills.** Colleges value students who work because it demonstrates responsibility and maturity. The skills you gain will also help you move up the ladder so that the next job you have will be better.

■ **Read that list of books your English teacher handed out.** Doing this will not only give you a head start on the fall but will also help you prepare for the standardized tests.

■ **Volunteer in your community.** Colleges like to see students who are involved and give back. Plus, think of the sense of satisfaction you'll feel from teaching an elementary school kid how to read or making the life of a senior less lonely.

■ **Take a summer school class at your high school or a community college.** You can do this to review material from a class that you didn't do as well in or to get a jump start on your classes for the fall. The biggest question that college admission officers ask when reviewing your application is: Will you be able to handle the academic courses at their college? Show that you will by taking a class.

You still have lots of days to be lazy or sleep in, so find a balance.

(3) Start on that college essay NOW.

College essays (as you'll see in Chapter Four) can be extremely influential in getting admitted to colleges. Don't wait until you have to actually write one; work on the basics you will need to know now. It would be like waiting until the homecoming game to work on your tackling or waiting until the debate tournament to think about what position you are taking on an issue.

Brush up on basic English skills and start thinking about what ideas you might want to write on. Refer to the sample questions listed in Chapter Four and think about how you would answer each one. Go to the library and check out a book on writing a quality and winning college essay. Read the samples to get a feel for what admission officers seem to prefer. Think how you would approach the same or similar topic. Line up your reasons, examples and anecdotes now, not later.

(4) Get to know your guidance counselor.

For many students, the guidance counselor is just one of those people in the background of your high school life. You rarely see him or her except on special occasions (or if you are in trouble). You have time to change that though. Schedule a visit with your guidance counselor. Ask for tips on how to increase your chances of getting into colleges. Ask for help in searching for some of the best options. This is a person who is there to help you, so make yourself accessible. Ask questions. Follow up on advice.

(5) Shed the fluff and take advanced placement, honors or college prep courses.

A number of colleges will do something with your GPA that you might not be aware of. They will look at the classes you took in high school, throw out the "fluff" classes and recalculate the "core" classes. Journalism, shop, drama, home economics—all gone. Only science, math and English remain. For many students, this is an unpleasant surprise because the grades they got in their elective classes were the ones responsible for driving up their overall GPA. Knowing this, you might want to choose different classes for your junior and senior years. Throw out the easy classes and take advanced placement or college prep courses instead (Suggestions: algebra, geometry, foreign languages, laboratory science and English.) The honest fact is that a B in a core class will gain you more than an A in any fluff class.

Patrick O'Brien adds, "Junior year for many is like boot camp, or to say it another way, it's more like college while the frosh and sophomore years are more like middle school. It is a breakthrough year with greater opportunities but also greater challenges. More self-direction is expected," he adds. "You should expect it of yourself. Keep all things in balance."

Mark Campbell, vice president for enrollment management at McKendree College, advises high school students, "Don't be tempted to take the soft senior year. Continue to develop your writing!"

Here is a helpful chart for converting your grades over to the point system used for computing GPAs.

A	4.0
A-	3.7
B+	3.3
B	3.0
B-	2.7
C+	2.3
C	2.0
C-	1.7
D+	1.3
D	1.0
D-	.7
F	0.0

(6) Get involved in your community with passion.

Another big influence on getting accepted into college is your history of being actively involved in your community in some way or another. Don't wait until your senior year summer to do this. Start looking around now for ways to play a part in your community but not just in a way to impress the admission departments. Do it to learn and explore, and find out more about yourself. Do it because it is a topic of great interest to you. Do it for passion not to look good on a piece of paper. You will be able to write or talk about that passion later in your essay or interview.

To find out more about advanced placement classes and programs, check out the website www.collegeboard.com/student/testing/ap/about.html.

Some possible places to get involved include volunteering at:

- schools

- crisis intervention centers

- homeless shelters

- park and recreation centers

- community gardens

- nursing homes

- libraries

- hunger relief centers

- humane society

- theatres

(7) Get a coach, tutor, mentor and/or study buddy.

Just like it is better to study several days before a test rather than several hours (or minutes), why wait to find someone who can help you succeed in so many ways? If you are not doing well in a class, do not hesitate to ask for help. Talk to your teachers. Get a tutor. Find a student to study with. Hire a coach. Learn from a mentor. Do what you need to do now to increase those grades, as well as your own enthusiasm, dedication and passion.

If the term mentor is new to you, here is some helpful information. A mentor can be a friend, coach, tutor, teacher, counselor or even a relative. Research has shown that mentoring relationships can help students to develop work ethics and a sense of responsibility, as well as help raise self-esteem, increase communication skills and improve personal relationships. The skills that mentors can teach you will most likely help in high school and certainly in college.

(8) Make sure you aren't working around a learning disability.

If you have been continually struggling in school and it has been showing up in your grades and test scores, make sure that you have been checked for any possible learning disability. It is possible that you have an undiagnosed issue that has given you a different learning style. Talk to your guidance counselor or family physician. Many of the colleges today welcome students with various learning disabilities. They have special programs geared especially for them.

The Top Five Facts about Learning Disabilities

When someone has a learning disability, what he or she should be able to do is different from what he or she is able to do. Learning disabilities are an invisible, life-long condition. You can't tell by looking at a person that he or she has one and learning disabilities can't be cured. One in every ten people has a Learning Disability.

A learning disability may mean you have difficulty with:

- spoken language
- written language
- coordination
- self-control
- organizational skills
- attention, or
- memory

FACT 1: People with LD are smart. People with LD have average to above average intelligence. Some people prefer to think of LD as a "different learning style" or a "learning difference." That's because you CAN learn, but the way in which you learn is different. You have a unique learning style.

FACT 2: There are many types of LD. *Dyslexia* is usually thought of as a reading disability although it also means having problems using language in many forms.

Dyscalculia causes people to have problems doing arithmetic and understanding math concepts. Many people have issues with math, but a person with dyscalculia has a much more difficult time solving basic math problems. *Dysgraphia* is a writing disorder that causes people to have difficulty forming letters or writing within a certain space. *Dyspraxia* is a problem with the body's system of motion. Dyspraxia makes it difficult for a person to control and coordinate his or her movements. *Auditory memory and processing disability* describes problems people have in understanding or remembering words or sounds because their brains don't understand language the way typical brains do.

FACT 3: LD is hereditary. No one knows the exact cause of LD but it is believed to be a problem with the central nervous system, meaning it is neurological. LD also tends to run in families. You may discover that one of your guardians or grandparents has trouble at school. LD is not caused by too much sugar, guardians who aren't strict enough or allergies.

FACT 4: LD must be assessed by a psychologist. Diagnosing LD involves a number of things. You and your guardians will be interviewed to find out what kind of problems you have had, how long you have had them and how seriously they have affected you. Your teachers should be interviewed as well.

You will be given several tests. These aren't the same kind of tests you take in school. Instead, the person testing you will ask your questions and get you to complete certain tasks. Once the tests are finished, the examiner looks at how you are doing at school and compares that with how you should be doing given how smart you are (your intelligence). If there is a difference between these that can't be explained by other reasons, then a diagnosis of LD is often made.

FACT 5: There is no cure for LD but lots can be done to help. One of the most important things you can do to help yourself is to understand what your particular LD is. It is also important for you to recognize and work on your strengths. Your guardians and teachers will help you learn about how to cope with your learning problems better by teaching strategies that can minimize their effect.

Source: Reprinted with permission from the Learning Disabilities Association of BC South Vancouver Island Chapter, www.know-yourrights.ca.

Not sure what qualifies as a learning disability? It's a blanket term that covers everything from not being able to sit still in class to not being able to read very well. There are many people who firmly believe that learning disability is the wrong term. Instead of a disability, it is simply just another way of learning material that is not like most people's. Review this important information about learning disabilities from an organization called Know Your Rights. Do you see yourself in this anywhere?

Worried that learning disabilities will interfere with your education? There are many successful people who have LD such as Whoopi Goldberg, Magic Johnson, Nelson Rockefeller, Jay Leno and Charles Schwab. Not too shabby, eh? Would you mind being on this list?

(9) Take classes at your local junior college.

Start your college career while you are still in high school by taking classes at your local junior or community college. Many of these institutions are very open to the idea. Terry O'Banion, former president of the League for Innovation in the Community College, explains the possibilities. "In the last decade or so, many high schools and community colleges have created articulated programs to allow students enrolled in high school to take courses for community college credit," she says. "Called 'dual or concurrent enrollment,' the practice is very widespread and is likely to expand in the next few years.

"The practice emerged because able high school students often exhaust the supply of solid courses by their senior year; there is no reason to wait until they graduate from high school to begin taking college-level courses," adds O'Banion. "Additionally, community colleges and high schools in the same region share common purposes of preparing students for the workforce or for further education, and they can enhance that purpose by creating opportunities for high school students to take courses at the local community college to round out their schedules," she concludes.

Tonia Johnson, associate director of admission at Guilford College, also discourages students from leaving school early in their senior year. Just because you have all the credits you need, use this time to do something that will impress admission officers. "Take courses somewhere, get involved in an internship, but use the time wisely," she says.

Regardless of the stage at which you need to make changes, don't look back at your mistakes, look forward to your possibilities. Making that difference can be enough to get your admission application placed in the accepted pile instead of that other stack. Write out the top ten list of changes, pin it up and give it the attention it needs. You might be surprised at the results!

SECTION 2

<u>GETTING IN</u>

Beyond the Basic Application Form: Explaining Weaknesses and Building on Strengths

CHAPTER THREE

• • • • • • • • • •

GPAs, SATs and ACTs, Oh My!

Let's face it. If you're reading this book, it means those wonderful acronyms in the title of this chapter are not your strong point. For one reason or another, your overall GPA or your test scores are just not that remarkable.

What can you do about that? One possibility is to check out the colleges that do not require standardized test scores as part of their admission process. What? you ask in amazement. There are colleges that don't want those all important numbers? That's right. In fact, there are more than 700 of them and they can be found at www.fairtest.org.

Why would some colleges choose not to rely on ACT and SAT scores? Here is how FairTest explains it:

> *"Test scores are biased and unreliable.* Standardized college admission tests are biased, imprecise and unreliable, and therefore should not be required for any college admission process or scholarship award. If test scores are optional, students who feel that their strengths are reflected by their SAT or ACT scores can submit them, while those whose abilities are better demonstrated by grades, recommendations, a portfolio or a special project are assured that these will be taken into full account. Sometimes admission officers use low test scores to automatically reject qualified candidates without even considering their schoolwork. That's simply not fair.
>
> *"Test scores are nearly useless in college admission.* Research shows that the SAT and ACT do not help colleges and universities make significantly better admission decisions. The University of Chicago Press book, *The Case Against the SAT* found that the SAT is 'statistically irrelevant' in college admission. It

also proves that the SAT undermines the goal of diversity by reducing the number of qualified minority and lower-income students who are admitted.

If you are applying to a school that requires SAT or ACT scores, Fair Test encourages you to ask some important questions including:

■ How does your school use the SAT and/or ACT?

■ Are cut-off scores used, in violation of College Board and ACT guidelines? If so, do they apply to general admission or to particular programs?

■ Does your school use any statistical formula which includes SAT/ACT scores to judge applicants' academic records?

■ Do they take possible coaching into account when considering ACT or SAT scores?

■ How does your college report SAT and ACT scores in handbooks and brochures?

■ Does it report simple averages or a range of scores?

Some Thoughts from College and University Officials on the SAT and ACT

"Schools that use the SAT are throwing away a third of their talent."
—William Hiss, dean of enrollment at Bates College

"While this test has some ability to predict student performance in the first year of college, it falls far short of predicting overall academic or career success and a host of other aptitudes that educators and society value, such as intellectual curiosity, motivation, persistence, leadership, creativity, civic engagement and social conscience."
—Joanne Creighton, president of Mount Holyoke College

"The negative impact of the SATs falls disproportionately on African Americans and Latinos. If you are about things like diversity in your student body, the SAT can be an impediment."
—Christopher Hooker-Haring, dean of admission at Muhlenberg College

Reprinted with permission of FairTest (www.fairtest.org)

- Does it include all entering students' scores in these figures, in compliance with the Good Practice Principles of the National Association for College Admission Counseling?

So, if all of this is true, why do most colleges rely so heavily on the results from standardized tests? If you think about it, an A at a high school in Chicago may be different than an A at a high school in Los Angeles. In fact, an A at two high schools in the same school district or even with two different physics teachers at the same high school may be different. Because schools have varying ways of awarding grades and varying levels of difficulty, colleges need a uniform way to measure students. The SAT and ACT have become those measures.

In recent years, test prep has become more than just an option. It's a booming business! During the last few years, it has grown from $100 million to more than triple that. More and more students are putting out big bucks to prepare themselves to take the SAT.

So while standardized tests may be unreliable and not every college requires them, it doesn't look like they are going away anytime soon. If you are applying to a college that requires test scores, then you have little choice but to "bite the bullet" and take the test.

Meet the New Tests

As you probably know, the SAT and ACT themselves have gone through changes recently. Here is what the new exams look like:

SAT Reasoning Test (www.collegeboard.com)

- The exam has three sections—Critical Reading, Math and Writing—each scored between 200 and 800 points for a total possible score of 2400.

- The Critical Reading section is 70 minutes long with two 25-minute sections and one 20-minute section. It contains reading comprehension, sentence completion and paragraph-length critical reading sections. This section replaces the old verbal section.

- The Math section is 70 minutes long with two 25-minute sections and one 20-minute section. It contains multiple-choice questions and student-produced responses on numbers and operations, algebra, geometry and statistics, probability and data analysis.

■ The Writing section contains a 25-minute essay that is first and a 35-minute multiple choice section that has questions on identifying sentence errors, improving sentences and improving paragraphs.

ACT (www.actstudent.org)

■ This exam has four multiple-choice tests and an optional Writing test. There is a score for each of the four tests (English, Math, Reading and Science) from 1 (low) to 36 (high), and the composite score is the average of the four test scores between 1 and 36.

■ The English section has 75 questions in 45 minutes that test standard written English (punctuation, grammar and usage, sentence structure) and rhetorical skills (strategy, organization, style).

■ The Mathematics section has 60 questions in 60 minutes that test pre-algebra (23 percent), elementary algebra (17 percent), intermediate algebra (15 percent), coordinate geometry

---

How Will My SAT Essay Be Graded?

Each essay will be scored independently by two high school and college teachers. Neither scorer will know what the other one gave. Each reader will assign the essay a score ranging from 1 to 6. Essays with a 6 are outstanding, with few to no errors at all. The main point of the essay has good support with stories, examples and reasons. It is organized, focused, coherent, smooth and uses a wide vocabulary.

■ A score of 5 means that the essay is effective, without being stellar. It is effective with only a few grammar/usage/mechanics errors.

■ Four means that the essay is competent, with some gaps in quality.

■ Three means that the essay is adequate but has a number of errors, including grammar/usage/mechanics, vocabulary, focus or development.

■ Two means that the essay is seriously limited with a number of weaknesses.

■ One means that the essay is severely flawed.

For more detailed information on how the scoring is done, check out the College Board website at www.collegeboard.com.

(15 percent), plane geometry (23 percent) and trigonometry (7 percent).

■ The Reading section has 40 questions in 35 minutes that test reading comprehension.

■ The Science section has 40 questions in 35 minutes that test the "interpretation, analysis, evaluation, reasoning and problem-solving skills" of natural sciences.

■ The optional Writing section has one essay prompt in 30 minutes that tests writing skills.

Tips for Getting a Higher Score

It goes without saying that doing well on the standardized tests (ACT/SAT) helps you get in the front door. There are dozens of books to tell you how to do well on these standardized tests, so I will not attempt to do it here. Instead, here's a quickie list of the most basic things you can do to assure you do the best you can:

■ Make a decision that the test is important to you and that you will give it time and effort.

■ Get familiar with the test format so it is not a surprise. Know what it will cover. You can get free sample exams from the creators of the exams at www.collegeboard.com for the SAT and www.act.org for the ACT.

■ Consider hiring a coach or tutor to help you prepare for the tests. There are intensive test preparation courses available from companies like Princeton Review (www.review.com) and Kaplan (www.kaplan.com), but there are also lower-cost options from community colleges and maybe even your high school.

■ Go to the library or bookstore and start looking at all the test prep books. They come in all formats. A recent trend is exciting novels of all kinds that entertain you while they introduce you to all of the vocabulary words you need to know for the test. Check the stories out at www.amazon.com or use a search engine to find "vocabulary SAT novels." The stories are so captivating, you completely forget that you are learning at the same time. SAT and ACT prep books are easy to find and will demystify the process for you.

■ Check out websites on the Internet for test help. Just put "SAT test preparation" in the search box. Here are just a few of the many out there:

www.review.com

www.kaplan.com

www.testprepreview.com

www.number2.com

www.act-sat-prep.com

A Word About Test Anxiety

Feeling worried or pressured about taking a test is normal. Indeed, a slight edginess can often enhance your performance. However, if the worry turns into panic and/or fear and makes it almost impossible to study or take the test, you probably are suffering from test anxiety.

Test anxiety can strike before and/or during a test. It can make you feel physically sick, from a headache or nausea to faintness and hyperventilating. You might have a dry mouth, pounding heart or sweaty hands or be unusually emotional. It is often very difficult to concentrate at all.

How can you combat it? Here are some tips:

1. **Be prepared as much as possible for the test.**

2. **Take good care of yourself.** Get enough sleep, eat healthy and get some regular exercise. Don't have any coffee before the test because caffeine increases your level of anxiety.

3. **Learn how to relax.** Sounds simple, but it can be challenging when your body and mind are trying to do just the opposite. Like with other things, practice is the key. Spend time learning how to think about each muscle group in your body. Start with your feet. Tighten them and then let them go. Work your way all the way up to your head. Breathe slowly and deeply.

4. **Replace negative thoughts with positive ones.** Instead of telling yourself, "I am just going to blow this entire test, I know it", say, "This may be a difficult test but I will do the best I can on it." Visualize yourself doing well on the test.

5. **When you are taking the test, remember those deep, slow breaths.** Be sure to read the test directions carefully. If you don't know a question, skip it and go back later.

6. **If you find yourself tensing up during the test, put down your pencil, take a few deep breaths, relax your neck and shoulders and then go back to it.**

7. **When you are done, do something fun.** See a movie, go out to eat, meet with a friend or just take a well-deserved nap.

www.4tests.com

www.petersons.com/testprepchannel

A last bit of advice before you take one of these standardized tests. Do not attempt to cram for them; it will never work. This is not that type of test. Instead go into the test well rested, following a good breakfast. Take the entire three hours and 35 minutes to complete it. Don't rush. If you get done early, just take the time to go back over it. Don't panic when you see other students turning in their tests when you are far from done. Everyone has a different learning pace and getting done faster is not an indication of how anyone did on the test. Know that you did the best you could and despite the scores, forge ahead. Colleges are waiting for you!

Taking the Credit, Taking the Blame

There will come a time within the application, essay or interview where you will be expected to either explain or discuss your SAT/ACT score and GPA. It's better to offer an explanation than to ignore your scores or GPA and hope that the admission officers don't notice them. In fact, they will notice them and without an explanation will have no reason to give you the benefit of the doubt.

Remember that admission officers are human beings. They have made mistakes or struggled in some way in their lives. They will understand and listen, so take the time to explain honestly why you believe your numbers are not as high as you had hoped they would be.

Here is a list of the general do's and don'ts that you need to remember when discussing your less than stellar numbers. The key is to be honest at all times.

DO: Explain any circumstances that affect your numbers such as:	**DON'T:**
frequent moves	whine
test anxiety or health issues	complain
learning disabilities	place blame on others (parents, teachers, etc.)
part-time jobs	adopt a "poor me" attitude
extenuating personal or family issues	be emotional

As you can see, it's important to take responsibility for your performance. Instead of making excuses or blaming others, state the facts and own up to how you did. There are legitimate and understandable reasons for not doing as well as you are capable of such as those listed above. Not having a date to the spring formal is not a good reason.

Also have a balance between providing enough information to make your case but not so much information that your explanation is overwhelming. For example, you might write that having a severely ill parent affected your ability to concentrate on your studies for a semester, but you don't need to also provide the detail of every medical procedure your parent has had.

If your grades are low in a specific subject, explain this. You can describe how you have sought extra help in the subject or how you took a summer school class to make sure you really understood the material, but it's still a weak area. You can also explain that you plan to major in another subject area in college in which you are stronger.

It's important as well to note any progress that you've made. If you have since improved your grades in a subject area or overall, indicate this and explain that you have a renewed commitment to your studies.

Once you have discussed this topic, you can move on to focus on your strengths instead. Without dwelling on the negative, you have the opportunity to highlight how much you have to offer the college.

Include a Resume to Highlight What You <u>Have</u> Accomplished

Many colleges will let you submit a resume. You may already have one on hand thanks to summer job searches that can act as your foundation. The resume you used for looking for a summer part-time job might give you some quality information to use, but it most likely will need changes before you share it with a college. Why? Two reasons: one, time has most likely passed since you wrote it and there may be new things to add and two, your intention is different. You aren't trying to impress some employer into giving you a weekly paycheck. This time, the goal is to impress a college admission officer and help you get through the front door of the school.

Resumes are like the Cliffs Notes of your academic/educational and community life. They are the condensed version of the great stuff you have accomplished in your life thus far. Resumes can be very effective.

Here are some tips for before you even start gathering the information:

- Have high-quality paper.

- Choose a font size and style that is easy to read (at least 12 and below 18 and Arial, Times New Roman, Garamond or Franklin Gothic Book.)

- Do not handwrite this resume. Even if you have to use the school or library computer, make sure this is neat and looks professional.

- Many word processing programs include a built-in resume wizard, so check and see if you can find one. This template walks you right through where to put what and then puts it in a format that looks great.

Here is what you need to include on your resume:

- full name

- current address

- telephone number (home and cell)

- email address

- all awards or honors you have earned

- all forms of community service

- all part-/full-time jobs

- references

- sports and extracurricular involvement—remember these can be outside of school as well!

One of the most important aspects of the resume is to include the pertinent details that truly explain what you have accomplished. For example, if you worked as a volunteer at a local children's day care center, include how many children you worked with and what responsibilities you held. This is the place where you can really shine in ways that your numbers do not reflect.

On the next page is an example of a typical type of resume you might want to include in your application:

123 4th St.
Anytown, USA 10000

Phone 555-555-5555
Fax 555-555-5556
E-mail anystudent@aol.com

Chris Smith

Community Involvement

Volunteered for six months (2004) at The Boys and Girls Club: helped organize and guide 30 children between the ages of 8 and 13 in multiple after-school activities. Learned skills of organization, teamwork, cooperation and discipline.

Intern at Wheels Unlimited, my grandfather's bicycle repair shop, after school for two years (2002-2004). Learned how to serve customers, run a register and basic mechanics/engineering skills.

Extracurricular Activities

Participated in the Chess Club (2002) and the Debate Club (2003-2004). Director of the Drama Club (2003) and President of the Ski Club (2005).

Employment

June-August 2003 20 hours a week at Marin County Public Library

June-August 2004 18 hours a week at the Community Theatre

Education

2002-2005 East County High School

Summer 2003 Theatre Workshop

Summer 2004 Sign Language 101 at St. Martin's Community College

References

Mr. Bob Smith, Youth Coordinator at the Boys and Girls Club, 555-222-1111

Mrs. Jean Youngblood, English/Language Arts Teacher, East County High School, 555-982-1120

Mr. Rod Cooper, High School Debate Coach, 555-888-1210

Miss Lindsay Francis, Professor of Sign Language, St. Martin's Community College, 555-333-0101

Awards received

Debate Team Regional First Prize, 2002

First Place, State Library Essay Contest, 2003

Heart of Gold, Volunteer Ribbon, 2004

After you have done all this hard work, don't blow it by not checking your spelling and grammar. The greatest resume will make a rotten impression if it has errors. Have someone else other than you go over it before you finalize it. They may catch a mistake you missed—or remember something wonderful you did that you forgot to include.

A resume gives the opportunity to share with the college more than your grades and test scores. It gives them a snapshot of your achievements that will really help them understand what you have to offer.

CHAPTER FOUR
. . . .

Winning in Writing: The All-Important College Essay

Not every college requires an essay, but most of them want to see one. If you are applying at one of the colleges that do not require ACT or SAT scores, for example, the college essay is extremely important. Bottom line: The chances are pretty good you will have to write an essay. And, putting aside your fears for a moment, that is a good thing.

For many admission officers, your essay is the first chance they get to see the real you. They already know your grades, test scores and what classes you have taken for the last four years, but they don't know YOU. Sure, they are looking at how well you remember those grammar and punctuation rules, as well as what kind of vocabulary you use, but they also want to glimpse your personality, your ambitions, talents, goals and dreams.

College essays have become such an important part of the admission process that there are many books dedicated to showing you how to write one, along with giving samples to read from accepted students. One excellent book is *Accepted! 50 Successful College Admission Essays*. Check out the many websites on the Net dedicated to the topic.

Be aware there are unscrupulous companies and people willing (for a price) to take the headache out of your hands and write the essay for you. Yes, you can buy your college essay. Is this ethical? What do you think? Not only is this wrong but it won't help you get into college. Purchased essays are never able to convey the real you to a college. Don't ask a friend or relative to write it for you either. The admission officers are good at spotting styles that don't fit with students. Not to mention that if you turn in a perfect paper, but your GPA in English classes has always been a B or less, a red flag will pop up immediately.

TYPICAL ESSAY QUESTIONS

■ Describe your most significant personal experience. Why was it significant and how has it influenced you?

■ Identify and discuss a significant problem facing your generation.

■ What have you read that has had a special significance to you? Explain why.

■ Describe a person or experience of particular importance to you.

■ Describe the reasons that influenced you in selecting your intended major field of study.

■ If you could travel through time and interview a prominent figure in the arts, politics, religion or science, for example, whom would you choose and why?

■ Describe your experience in living in a racially, culturally or ethnically diverse environment; what do you expect to need to know to live successfully in the multi-cultural society of the future?

■ Make up a question, state it clearly and answer it. Feel free to use your imagination, recognizing that those who read it will not mind being entertained.

■ Indicate what you consider your best qualities to be and describe how your college education will be of assistance to you in sharing these qualities and your accomplishments with others.

■ Evaluate a significant experience, achievement or risk that you have taken and its impact on you.

■ Indicate a person, character in fiction, an historical figure or a creative work (as in art, music, etc.) who has had a significant influence on you and describe that influence.

■ Why do you want to spend two to six years of your life at a particular college, graduate school or professional school? How is the degree necessary to the fulfillment of your goals?

■ Use this space to let us know something about you that we might not learn from the rest of your application.

■ How have you grown and developed over the four years of your high school career?

■ What is the biggest risk you have ever taken?

■ Discuss some issue of personal, local or national concern and why it is important to you.

■ Write about your favorite book or film and tell why it has influenced you.

- Relate the most humorous experience in your life.

- You have just finished writing your 300-page autobiography. Please submit page 217.

But the best reason for writing your own essay is that regardless of your skill you can write a successful essay. It's not as hard as you might imagine! Read on to learn how.

The question you are given to write about in a college essay ranges a great deal. Regardless of the question, the point is to say who you are. You will show that in how you respond, what anecdotes you use, what examples you include and so on.

Essay Mistakes to Avoid from the Get Go

There are some pitfalls you need to avoid in your essay. Since this is your chance to sound unique and individual, don't respond with the answers that everyone else does. For example, if you are asked to write about a book you have read, don't pick the one that all high school students were forced to read. Pick something unusual or different. It does not matter if the admission officer has ever heard of it. What matters is how you explain why it was an important book to you.

If you are asked to write about an event in your life, go beyond just describing it. Show how it affected your life, how you are different because of it. The trick here is not writing what everyone else does. Along with Dr. Seuss essays, admission officers weary of reading essays that focus on the "I've seen the light" philosophy. You lost the game, but achieved a goal. Your parents got divorced/took drugs and it taught you a lesson. You had this favorite teacher or coach. It's one thing to write about something that you learned from the experience, but it's over the top to write that you've found the purpose of life through these experiences. It's easy to think that you have to be profound and philosophical when you write this essay, but the truth is admission officers see more than enough of that.

Other things to avoid:

Don't try to be cute by adding poetry or illustrations unless they directly relate to your topic or your specific talent; don't use unusually fancy paper; never handwrite the essay. While it is okay to be emotional, do not whine, complain or be sarcastic. Avoid using current films, actors or television shows for your examples, and don't try to sell yourself. Represent the special person you are, but don't sound like an overzealous salesman working on commission. Don't use anyone else's idea even if it is interesting. It won't sound like you and your support will sound hollow.

Be funny; be enthusiastic; be reflective—but make sure it is not something that you and 4,000 other students wrote about. Go beyond the expected and you will get noticed. The college essay is often the deciding factor at some colleges in whether you are accepted or rejected. You want your words to push you over the top.

Putting Words on Paper

College essays are typically 250 to 500 words. That is about one to two pages of typing, double spaced. According to the Common Application (www.commonapp.org), that limit is a guideline because colleges do not actually count the words. They won't mind if it is a little shorter or longer because quality is far more important than quantity. "College admission officers are far more concerned that the essay is well written, proofread (not just spell-checked), well thought out, etc. Do not get caught up in the 'micro' (words, spacing, font size, color of ink)," states the website. "They are looking for the 'macro': does the student write well and what can they learn about this person from his/her essay?" Their website has more helpful information on what you will find on the most commonly used college application forms.

Once you know the question, sit down and brainstorm possible answers. Just let your mind wander around the topic and write it all down without judgment or self-censorship. When you have run out of ideas,

This is Your Chance!

Quite often, the college application essay is the perfect opportunity to tackle the subject of your less-than stellar quality test scores or GPA. Many times you can tie the question you are asked to write about to the subject of your strengths and weaknesses. If you directly address the issue in your essay, do so. Look back over the list of the most commonly asked questions. Can you see how you could relate your strengths to the topic? For example, how about "Use this space to let us know something about you that we might not learn from the rest of your application"? You could explain how you have been persistent, dedicated, strong, determined, creative or any other admirable trait through examples. You can show the admission officers that while your numbers may not be the strongest they have seen, you apparently are a bright, skilled and wonderful student that would be an excellent addition to any college. Think of the essay as your time to shine!

start going through what you have. What looks best? Throw out the things you could only write a paragraph about. Look for the ones that make you feel emotional; that probably means they impacted your life in some way. Choose one.

Now, write out an outline, just like you have done for other papers and reports you've done in school. What are the main points you want to cover? What details go under each point? For example, imagine that you have been asked to write about something you have read that was significant to you. Some points you might want to cover include: Why you chose to read the book, how you felt while reading it, what new perspectives or points of view it taught you, what questions it raised in your mind, what you learned from the experience.

Once your outline is done, it is time to write your first draft (and yes, that means there will be second, third and more drafts before you're done). Do not start your essay with any of the following opening sentences:

- My name is Kevin Jones and I …

- I was born in Los Angeles, California, and …

- My college admission essay is going to be about …

- I am writing this because I really want to go to your college…

- This is the story of my life so far …

- I am such a great person you will want to read my story …

- My parents, Jean and Jasper Carpenter, first moved …

They are boring and you will most likely have lost the reader's attention in the very first paragraph. Lead with something interesting, eye-catching and unique. Grab the admission officer's attention by writing something that will make him or her put down that cup of coffee, sit up straight in the chair and want to read what comes next.

Your first draft should be written without worrying about grammar, spelling or punctuation. You want to get your best thoughts down first, without being slowed down by rules. In case you don't remember the basic structure from endless English classes, you need the minimum of a five-paragraph essay. It should look pretty much like this:

INTRODUCTION thesis statement
BODY: Paragraph 2 support for thesis statement
BODY: Paragraph 3 support for thesis statement
BODY: Paragraph 4 support for thesis statement
CONCLUSION summary of main points

When you are done, show the first draft to your friends and family. Ask their opinions. Should you give more detail? Was everything clear? Did it represent your personality? Is this how they would have imagined you answered the question? Listen carefully to their feedback so you can use it in your revisions.

Now write a second draft, pulling in any extra details you remembered and keeping others' comments in mind. This time around, fix any spelling, grammar or punctuation errors. Share it with a favorite teacher or your guidance counselor. Get their comments. Go back to the desk. Go through it again, keeping the new feedback in mind. Run spell check (but do not depend on it) and print. You're ready.

What If I'm Not a Writer?

It is entirely possible that you are a whiz at math or a mad scientist and writing just isn't your forte. If this is true, the college essay may be all that much more intimidating. So let's give your essay some thought before you begin to put words on paper.

Here are some ways to take your brilliant ideas and eventually come up with an essay. Which one sounds best to you?

- Get a tape recorder and speak what you would like to have in your essay. Consider this your first draft. Listen to it and re-fine it and when it centers on what you want to say, either type it up as you listen or ask someone else to transcribe it for you.

■ Sit down and talk to your parents or a special friend about your response to the essay question or topic. As you speak, have that person make a list or an outline of what points you mention. Once you have a basic roadmap, it can be easier to start writing the essay.

■ Find some friends who are writers and ask for their tips, ideas and suggestions. Have one of them tutor you through the process as you write the essay.

■ Get some books from the library that have sample essays and see if you can use them as inspiration.

■ Ask your English teacher for some guidance in putting your ideas on paper.

■ Check to see if the college you are applying to allows for some flexibility in the format of your essay. If so, you might be able to write it as a lab report or some other format that feels more comfortable to you. You might also see if a college will accept a verbal essay rather than a written one.

■ Write the essay as best you can and then let someone who writes very well go over it for suggestions, corrections and revisions.

Out of Your Hands

It is done, gone and out of your hands. What happens to your essay now? That depends on the college. At least one person will read your essay. At smaller, more intimate colleges, most likely it will be more than one. Quite often the first person to see it is an admission officer, commonly an alumnus of the college or someone with a strong background in education. If there are multiple readings, your essay passes next to another admission officer or perhaps a director. At some colleges, it will even be presented to an entire admission committee.

The college essay is important, so give it the time, attention and effort it deserves. In turn, the colleges will give your essay the time, attention and effort it deserves.

Winning in Admission—With Someone Else's Words

Another element of the admission process that is too important to overlook is the personal reference letters. This time you don't have to sell yourself with your words; other people's will do the job for you.

Whom should you ask to write a letter of reference? Common sense says to make it someone who likes you, right? Just don't make it your grandmother, best friend or boyfriend. Sure, they like you—even love you—but you need a letter that will show how a person has evaluated you as a potential student, not something about how you are the best granddaughter, friend or girlfriend in the world. Here are some potential people to ask:

- co-workers, employers or supervisors

- teachers

- coaches

- other school faculty

- if you have done volunteer work, ask the organization's leader

How do you go about asking for a letter of reference? Ask in person rather than by email or telephone. This way you can show how much it would mean to you to have their personal recommendation.

Be sure to give the person enough time. Don't walk up to your boss at the end of the shift and say, "Before I go home tonight, could you write a reference letter for me?" Ask weeks ahead, if possible. If there are word limits or other restrictions on the letter's format, be sure and tell the person before they begin writing.

Some people may not know how to write a personal reference letter, so be ready to tell them what it should include. Provide a resume or summary of some of your achievements to help them write the letter. And include a stamped, addressed envelope to the school. The typical letter will cover:

- Who the writer is

- What the writer's relationship is with you (teacher/student; employer/employee, etc.)

- Why you have chosen to recommend this person

- Examples and illustrations of the student's strong points

- An overall evaluation of the student

- A conclusion

- One to two pages in length

Afterwards, always, always, always show your appreciation and gratitude for their help. A thank you note is really good manners, but a direct and sincere thank you face to face is great too.

CHAPTER FIVE

· · · · · · · · ·

Winning in Words: The Also-Important College Interview

You may or may not have won them over with your written words, so now it's time to dazzle them with your verbal wit. The college interview is important too as it is another chance to show a school just who you are, why you want to attend their college and why they should count themselves lucky to get you (in a humble fashion, of course.) It is also another chance to explain why your numbers are not as high as they could be.

While not all colleges require an interview, if you are given the opportunity, take it. For most schools, you don't even have to travel far for the interview. They may be held at the school with an admission officer or even in your community by local alumni. It might be easier for you to discuss issues face to face, rather than on paper.

Of course, unlike the essay, this time you don't get the chance to brainstorm, outline, think about, mull over, ponder and weigh your responses. Your responses are going to be on the spot, so preparation is the key to not looking like a befuddled idiot desperately searching for the right answers.

What kinds of questions will you be asked at an interview? They are similar to the ones on the essay. But the essay has just one question to answer. In the interview, you typically answer a number of questions for 15 minutes to an hour. They are often divided up into categories like school/classes, teachers, extracurricular activities, community, college and the world. Here are some typical examples. As you read them, think about how you would answer.

- How would you describe your school?

- How do you fit into your school?

- If you could change one thing about your school, what would it be? Why?

- What has been your most/least favorite class in school?

- Who was your most/least favorite teacher in school?

- How do you spend your free time and/or summers?

- Do you have a hobby of some kind? Tell me about it.

- Why are you interested in coming to this college?

- Where do you see yourself four years from now?

- What would you like to change about yourself?

- What are the three words that best describe you?

- What accomplishment are you most proud of?

- Why do you think you are a good match for this college?

- What do you think about _____ (current event, literature, art, music or other contemporary subject)

Who will ask you these questions? It depends on the college. It may be an admission officer, another student or an alumnus.

How do I respond to questions like "Tell me about your greatest failure" or "What is your biggest weakness"?

Contrary to what it may seem, these are not trick questions. They ask you to examine yourself closely and be honest. Admission officers often ask them to help draw out meaningful experiences in your life and show you have coped with a variety of challenges. To prepare for a question like this, just think a moment about what kind of difficult moments you have had to deal with in your life. Did your parents get divorced? Did you lose a friend? Think about what you have had to struggle with. Did you have trouble with a certain subject? How did you overcome it? What personality trait gives you the most trouble? What do you do about it? When you answer a question like this, you may just find out some amazing things about yourself that you had not realized yet!

Don't Just Talk About You

Since the interviewers are real people, they value real conversations. What would you prefer: Listening to a one-hour soliloquy, with Socratic references, on the merits of academia as perceived through the eyes of an 18-year-old or participating in an intriguing conversation about current events, life experiences and personal opinions? Needless to say, interviewers prefer the latter.

Throughout your interviews, remind yourself that your goal is to achieve two-way conversation. Be careful of any interview where the subject is you and you dominate the interview talking about your accomplishments. Don't worry about trying to mention all your achievements—your interviewer will ask about them. At the same time, however, this is not the only thing the interview is about.

Common sense tells us that most people enjoy talking about themselves, and interviewers are no different. Your interviewers volunteered for this job because they enjoyed their college experience and they like talking to potential students. Interviewers are usually the kind of people who love to give advice to young prospects. Think of this as a time not only for your interviewers to learn about you but also for you to find out as much as you can about them and their experiences.

Reprinted with permission from *Get into Any College* by Gen and Kelly Tanabe

Keep in mind that a college interview is usually more like a casual chat over coffee, not a white light in your face interrogation. If you have a good sense of humor, now is the time to show it. If you have a talent, skill or ability that just did not fit on the application form or in your essay, speak now or forever hold your peace. If you can, find out if the interview is considered to be informational (just getting some facts about you and a time for questions and answers) or evaluative (part of the admission criteria).

If you're feeling nervous as you go into the interview, that is understandable. In a way, it is a good thing because it will give you that extra boost of adrenaline you need to keep on your toes and pay attention. A person who isn't at least a little bit nervous may not do as well as one who is!

To make this less of a stressful event, practice what you are going to say ahead of time. Entertain your friends and family with it. Do it in front of the mirror or to an understanding guidance counselor. Prepare an answer for all the possible questions so you are ready, no matter which one the officer may ask.

The bottom line of the interview is simple—it is not the end all, be all of the admission process. It will not usually make or break your acceptance. The person talking to you is a human being and may well have gone through the exact same thing you are going through right now. This means you will glimpse some compassion, empathy and even a smile during the interview. Relax, take a few deep breaths and let the special person that you are shine out!

According to the people a www.collegeboard.com, there are 13 things to avoid in a college interview. Are you paying attention? Here they are!

Don't:

- Be late

- Memorize speeches—sound natural and conversational

- Ask questions covered by the college catalog

- Chew gum

- Wear lots of cologne or perfume

- Swear or use too much slang

The Moment of Truth

What happens when the admission officer asks you, "How do you explain the fact that your SAT score or GPA is a little less than wonderful?" First, expect it. That way you can prepare for it. If it doesn't happen, then whew! off the hook. If it does, you're ready. Second, be honest. Don't say there was a computer error or you really did better than that. Third, don't place blame. Don't try and put those numbers off on rotten teachers, stupid tests or unfair grading. On the other hand, explain with a truthful assessment of factors affecting your life. Was there a crisis during that time? Did you have to work extra hours that cut into study time? Were you heavily involved with sports or other extracurricular activities? Did you find high school boring or stifling? Without accusing others, tell the interviewer why you believe those numbers do not represent your real potential.

What should you do if the admission officer does not ask about your numbers? That's a judgment call, and the answer rests on your gut instinct. If the interview has gone really well and you feel like you have good rapport with the officer, explaining those numbers without being asked to first can be seen as admirable. If you have not clicked with the officer, however, and the interview has had some awkward pauses, you might want to just skip this so things don't go downhill.

Your Interview Homework

Remember those college brochures filled with pictures, statistics and text cultivating dust balls under your bed? Dig them out before your interview and do something really radical—read them! It is not necessary to read them cover to cover, but knowing such basic facts as where the school is located, what kind of environment it has, some of the courses it offers and some of the activities you may choose to participate in is a good idea. It does not impress interviewers when they discover that students who are applying to their beloved alma mater do not even know what state it is located in or that the college is single sex. (There was an applicant who actually made it to the interview before he learned that the college he was applying to was an all-women school!)

Try to talk to relatives or friends who attend or have attended the college. They can give you insights into the college that are not found in the glossy brochures. The more you know the better.

Doing your homework will allow you to be able to ask intelligent questions. You are making the most important decision in your life so far. It makes sense that you would have a question or two about it. Having prepared questions not only helps create the two-way conversation dynamic, but it also demonstrates that you are serious about attending the college.

Not all questions are good questions, and in particular, avoid asking those obvious ones whose answers are on the first page of the college's brochure. Instead, the best questions to ask your interviewers are those that make them reflect on their own experience, require them to do a little thinking and elicit an opinion. Making your interviewers think or express their opinions makes the interviews more interesting for them and makes your question seem insightful and probing. Some examples:

- What do you think about the X department?

- How did the small/large class size affect your education?

- How did X college prepare you for your career?

- What was the best opportunity you felt X university provided you?

- What is the best/worst aspect of X university or X city?

- If you had to do it again, what would you do differently?

Think of some more and write them on a list with the most interesting ones at the top. Take this list into the interviews and refer to them when the conversation begins to stall and when your interviewers ask you if you have any questions.

Reprinted with permission from *Get into Any College* by Gen and Kelly Tanabe

> "Unless you show up in a T-shirt and cut-offs and spew profanities, chances are the interview is not going to make or break you. As long as you've prepared and practiced, you'll probably make a good impression."
>
> —Excerpt from www.collegeboard.com

- Be arrogant—there's a fine line between being confident and boasting

- Lie—it will come back to haunt you

- Respond with only "yes" or "no" answers

- Tell the school it's your safety or last choice

- Be rude to the receptionist or any other staff you meet

- Bring a parent into the interview

- Refuse an interview

During the interview, more than your words count. While you don't have to come to the interview in a suit and tie or a dress, you shouldn't show up in shorts and tank top either. Be professional in your appearance. As you talk to the interviewer, sit up straight, don't fidget and make eye contact. Never interrupt, and be sure to shake hands at the beginning and the end.

Your college interview is also your chance for you to ask questions. By doing so, you often show initiative and curiosity—two traits most colleges are looking for in their students. Ask if the officer has any advice for you, ask a question about your potential major, ask about dorm activities and college lifestyle. Find out if there will be a new student orientation program, what activities are available for freshmen, what part-time job opportunities there are in the area or end with a zinger like, "Is there anything you would like to know about me in order to help you make a fair and final decision about my application?"

The interview is a unique opportunity to establish rapport with a person who previously only knew you as numbers and words on paper. Use it wisely and show them what a fantastic person you really are!

SECTION 3

PAYING

B Students Can Win Scholarships

CHAPTER SIX
• • • • • • • •

B Students Can Win Scholarships Too

"My GPA is not that hot…and my SAT scores were lousy because I had a temperature/didn't get enough sleep/forgot to prepare/had an argument with my boyfriend, so I wonder if I can even get into college…But heck, college costs thousands and thousands of dollars and my family cannot afford that. Why even apply…My parents don't have the money and scholarships only go to the straight A students anyway…"

Have you had that conversation with yourself? If so, you aren't the first and certainly won't be the last. But be advised: Such thinking is a big mistake.

Without question college costs a lot, and most families struggle to find enough money to pay for it. But those scholarships you keep hearing about are not just for the eggheads or overachievers who excelled in everything from U.S. history to trigonometry.

So who exactly gets scholarships besides those with high numbers? Let's take a look.

Students who show genuine financial need

And you thought growing up without a Porsche in the driveway was a bad thing? Scholarships were originally set up for these very students. They were put into place to support students' families financially so that college could be possible for many more. If your family has a genuine need to help you attend college, many scholarships may be available for you. The key to snatching one of them is simple: be honest about ALL of your numbers; don't try to fudge those income levels because it is not honest and you will get caught. Also be prepared to show any extenuating circumstances behind those numbers. Was your mother laid off? Was there a medical emergency? Does your family have three kids in college already? These are important factors to include.

Myth: You need straight A's to win money for college

The Truth: While straight A's certainly don't hurt your chances of winning, you may be tempted to place too much importance on your grades. Many scholarships are based on criteria other than grades and awarded for specific skills or talents such as linguistic, athletic or artistic ability. Even for scholarships in which grades are considered, they are often not the most important factor. What's more important is that you best match the qualities the scholarship committee seeks. Most students who win scholarships do not have the highest GPA. Don't let the lack of a perfect transcript prevent you from applying for scholarships.

—Gen and Kelly Tanabe, *Get Free Cash for College*

Students with a disability or illness

Not that you would wish for one, but if you happen to have a documented disability or illness, here is a perk. A number of organizations support students with some kind of physical challenge. Scholarships are available from such sources as the Alexander Graham Bell Association, American Foundation for the Blind, Hemophilia Resources of America and the National Center for Learning Disabilities.

Students with specific majors

Already know what you want to do with the rest of your life? Countless organizations support young people who are pursuing certain careers. You must show that you are genuinely passionate about whatever field it might be, from digital photography to interior design. You will need to let the scholarship people know how you found out about the field, who mentored or inspired you, how your dedication grew and what skills you learned or developed. Have truthful, profound stories ready to share. Have you started your own business in this career already? Have you supported your fascination through volunteer work? Do you have recommendations from people in a related field? These are the factors that will help a committee select you above all others for that cash. Consider these examples: The American Nursery and Landscape Association has money for those who love flowers, trees and the outdoors. The Arabian Horse Foundation helps those who adore horses. Other organizations have money for those whose focus is cooking, construction, forestry, hospitality, the performing arts and more.

Students who show leadership

Are you known for taking charge and putting things together? Do you already have a few groupies that really like you? Scholarship committees are impressed with young people who have shown some form of leadership. If you have helped others through organization and guidance, if you have inspired others, then this is the place to speak up. What have you done? Show it, don't just tell it. Give concrete examples such as letters of recommendation, photographs and projects. Point out the responsibilities you have taken on and what they have taught you. Places like the Financial Service Centers of America, the Coca-Cola Scholars Foundation and Discover Card promote their own businesses by sharing their profits with students like you.

Students with particular religious backgrounds

If you have been wondering if God has been listening to those prayers, this might be your answer. To promote the growth and development of their religion, many church organizations offer students college scholarships. Okay, time for real honesty here. Do not try to get one of these if the only time you go to church is weddings, funerals and right before a major test. You have to be a true believer in the religion and show it through your active involvement with the church. Perhaps you led a youth group, worked in the church nursery, took classes from the pastor or other relevant actions. It is common to see scholarships from the Methodist, Catholic, Baptist and Presbyterian churches.

Students with superior athletic ability

Love to chase some kind of ball around? If you are the star football, basketball, baseball, tennis, golf or track star, chances are there is a college or organization that wants to give you the money to go to college. As Gen and Kelly Tanabe say in their book on scholarships, "Athletic scholarships are the Holy Grail. At their best, they can cover tuition and fees, room and board and books. That's not bad for doing something that you enjoy." Not sure if your sport is covered? Even the Ice Skating Institute of American Education Foundation and the National Archery Association have money to share.

Students with a specific ethnic background

Time to look through your family tree. To celebrate their history and culture, some ethnic organizations are willing to give you money for school. This helps increase the number of minorities on campuses and also encourages minorities to go into professions they might have ignored or overlooked otherwise. Many groups are represented including such organizations as the Sons of Norway and the National Italian American Foundation Scholarships.

Students with certain hobbies

And your friends tried to say you were wasting your time! Scholarships are out there for young people who have serious hobbies. Of course, you have to show that you don't just pursue this hobby on rainy weekend afternoons, but on a regular basis. You need to prove that you have improved and that this hobby has led you to awards and honors or even to your own business. Discuss how this hobby has affected your life and what skills it has taught you. Be sure to include letters of recommendation from people who have seen what you are capable of. Do you spend hours doing graphic design on your computer? Have you sold some of your original logos to local companies? The Rhythm and Hues Studios might have money for you. Is photography all you can think about? Have you had your own displays at local stores? Do people call you to take pictures at their weddings or parties? Have your shots already popped up in the community newspaper? Talk to the National Press Photographers Foundation.

Students with parents who have generous employers

Check out where mom and dad work. It is not uncommon for businesses and corporations to include in their employee package some scholarship money for workers' kids. Ask your parents to read through their employee handbooks again or just ask some questions. Who knows what might be there that no one thought about before?

I hope you're convinced by now that that just as colleges will happily take students with less-than-stellar grades and test scores, so will they just as happily take students who do not come from the wealthiest families. Financial aid is a huge part of college admission and one that often means you can get that education you once told yourself was way out of reach. It's time to start an all-new conversation with yourself, along the lines of, "Hey, colleges really DO like me, and my family really CAN afford it now. So, what am I waiting for?"

Where to Find Scholarships

For most students, the hunt for scholarships is a short one. Many start with a scholarship book or head to the Internet. Unfortunately, most students end their search after exhausting these two sources.

Big mistake!

Books and the Internet are only the tip of the iceberg, and neither comes close to listing all the available scholarships. If you do your own detective work and canvass the community, you will uncover additional awards. Here's where to begin:

High school. The first stop in your scholarship hunt should be the high school counseling office. When an organization establishes a new scholarship (awards are created every year), high schools are the first places to get a notice. Over the years, most counseling offices have assembled a long list of scholarships. Don't reinvent the wheel if the counselor has already collected the information.

Prospective colleges. Contact the financial aid office at every school you are interested in attending. Not only do the colleges themselves offer scholarships, but their financial aid offices also maintain lists of outside opportunities.

Civic and community organizations. Every community is home to dozens of civic organizations, such as the Rotary Club, Lions Club, Knights of Columbus, American Legion, Elks Club and VFW. Part of their mission is to support the community by awarding scholarships.

Businesses big and small. Many businesses—such as newspapers, shopping malls, supermarkets and retailers—offer scholarships to local students. For example, every Wal-Mart and Target store awards scholarships to students in the community. To find these opportunities, contact the manager at these businesses. You can get a list of businesses from the chamber of commerce or in the reference section of the public library.

Parent's employers/union. If your parents work for a large company, have them ask the human resources department about scholarships. If they are limited to the children of employees, there may be little competition for these awards. Also, if your parents are a member of a union, have them ask the union representative about scholarships.

Professional or trade associations. From accounting to zoology, every profession has its own associations, and many of these professional associations use scholarships to encourage students to enter the field. Start by looking at groups related to your future career.

Religious organizations. Your church or temple may offer scholarships to support members. If your local church does not have a scholarship program, check with the national headquarters.

Ethnic and cultural organizations. To promote a certain culture, develop leaders or encourage members to pursue higher education, many ethnic organizations sponsor scholarships.

State and local governments. Make those tax dollars work for you by taking advantage of financial aid from state and local governments. Each state has a higher education agency that provides information on financial aid, and many administer state-based grant and loan programs. Closer to home, your county or city government may have awards for students in the community.

Private foundations and charities. As part of their mission to help the community, private foundations and charities often offer scholarships. To find these scholarships, visit your library and ask the reference librarian for a directory of local charities and foundations.

Friends and family. The more people who know you are looking for scholarships, the better. Friends and family members can be invaluable scholarship scouts as they go about their daily business. Scholarship opportunities have been uncovered on supermarket bulletin boards, standing in line at a bank, even on a bottle of aspirin. You never know where a scholarship will be publicized and who can help you to find it.

The Internet. Thousands of scholarships are just a click away. Websites such as College Answer (www.collegeanswer.com) make it easy to find scholarships free-of-charge. Although the Internet is a valuable resource, it is not a magic solution. Remember to use all the resources available to you.

Reprinted with permission from *Sallie Mae How to Pay for College* by Gen and Kelly Tanabe.

SECTION 4

COPING

Tips for Thriving

CHAPTER SEVEN

• • • • • • • • • • •

What Is Due When: The Top Ten of Time Management

No matter how you feel about cloning, by the time you have been in college for a few months you will be a staunch fan of the concept. The possibility of being in two places at one time will sound like the perfect solution, if only it were possible.

For many of us, college is the very first time where we find ourselves with so much to do, so little time. Suddenly, 24 hours is simply not enough. You have classes, friends, homework, a hobby or two, perhaps sports practice or a part-time job. Oh, yes, and time for sleeping, eating and basic hygiene. Squeezing all that into a day is not just difficult, it can border on impossible. Help is on the way. In fact, here it is. Turn this list into your daily mantra.

What you need to realize about college life (and you will hear this over and over, so be prepared) is that all of a sudden responsibility is on you and you alone. Did you just grin…or gulp? Just imagine you are Spiderman and whisper, "With great power comes great responsibility." There are no parents to look over your shoulder and remind/nag you to get things done. Your professors will be too busy to notice what you are and are not doing. There is no one to report to, and no one is keeping track of your activities. If a project gets done, it's because you did it. If it doesn't, well, you know where the blame lies, right? It takes a combination of practice, dedication, organization and most of all self-discipline to make sure you cover everything. This is where you get to prove how grown up and mature you truly are. Are you ready? Here are some tips.

(1) So much work, so little time

Even if you are an English major and you only know enough basic math to balance your checkbook each month, take a minute and fiddle around with these numbers. Start with the standard 24 hours in each day. That's all you get, no matter who you know or what you do.

Write the numbers 1 to 24 on a piece of paper. Label 1 through 8 SLEEP. Certainly there will be times where your shuteye will be more or less, but use this as an average for now. Next look at your class schedule and figure out how many hours a day you are actually sitting in the classroom or lab. While that can change, let's say four hours a day for now. So you can label hours 9, 10, 11 and 12 SCHOOL. Mark 13, 14 and 15 EATING. Say you have a four-hour part-time job. Mark 16, 17, 18 and 19. You have five hours left for everything from sports practice, exercise and studying to hanging out with friends and those tedious duties like showering, brushing your teeth, changing clothes and doing laundry.

Can you see the problem? Too easily, we begin to rely on weekends to catch up on what we missed during the week. Unfortunately, those days are usually busier than weekdays. If your time is not carefully scheduled, something will get left out and too easily it will be the important things like homework and classes.

When it comes to scheduling things, remember Murphy's Law of Time: Time goes faster than you expect and everything takes longer than you think.

(2) Love your syllabus.

When you go to class and the professor hands out the syllabus, take a moment to focus your full attention on it. Appreciate it. Respect it. It is one of the most important things you will ever be given while you are in college. In virtually every syllabus, there is a list of what you will be expected to do for each week of class. It will list homework assignments, quizzes (except those dratted pop quizzes), reports and papers. Just think of it as a roadmap to consult repeatedly as you take off on a long journey so that you don't get lost.

Most syllabi contain other vital information as well, including sections on:

- where class is held

- how to contact the professor

- grading plan, i.e. how much depends on test scores, papers, etc.

- course description

- course objectives

- course topics

- required texts and supplies

- attendance requirements

- classroom rules of conduct

- class schedule of tests, quizzes, papers, projects and home-work assignments

You may think that heck, I don't need this silly old syllabus because the professor will remind us all when a test or paper is due, right? Not quite. That may have been the case in high school, but no longer. Classes are bigger, professors are busier. Many of them never say a word, expecting you to be responsible enough (there is that word again) to monitor what is due when. And let's face it, it is no fun to walk in to class and find out there is a test you didn't study for.

When you get back to your room, take out the syllabus and grab a highlighter or two. Go through each line and highlight those important due dates. Remember that if you have a test, you need to plan on time to study. If you have a paper, plan time for researching at the library or on the Internet, as well as hours for outlining and writing. Those steps have to be allotted for as well. Next, you will take the information from each one and put it into…tip three. (Great segue, eh?)

(3) Worship your day planner.

Even though you may have laughed at or even made fun of those people who always walk around with those nerdy day planners in their arms, you are about to join their ranks. A day planner is your key to managing time so let's take a look at what it can do for you.

The first step to creating a good day planner is to pick one you like. Head out to the office supply store or college bookstore and look through them. Does one appeal to you more than another? Does the shape and size feel right? Do you like plain or fancy? Lines or no lines? Make the day planner your own; add stickers, photos, drawings, whatever you need to personalize it. Whatever you like is fine, as long as it has a monthly or weekly calendar and pages for you to write out what you are going to do each day. If you want to take the high-tech route, an electronic planner works too.

Open up the day planner to the current month and write down all time commitments you have. Write them in pencil, however, so you can change things if necessary without making a scratched up mess. Be sure to include class time, work, any kind of practice, meeting with friends, study groups or other regular activities. Now add the due dates for your quizzes, tests, papers and projects. Do this for as many months as you have data for. It gives you an excuse to count how many days until spring break.

Writing it all down is a wonderful thing to do but meaningless if you do not open up and look at the day planner on a regular basis. Consult it multiple times a day to make sure that you are keeping up in everything. If a friend asks you to the movies, check the book. If you want to join a group that has regular meetings, look at the book. Carry the day planner with you wherever you go. Jam it in your backpack. Stick it in a pocket. Shove it in a purse. Got the point? Use it. Look at it. Live by it.

(4) You're on my list.

Do you remember all those lists your parents seemed to have around the house? Your mom may have made grocery lists or bills to be paid lists. Your dad might have made lists of what he needed to get from Home Depot. Maybe you have even kept lists of your favorite books or bands, your top ten movies or the foods you liked best in your sack lunches.

College is the perfect place to either start the list habit or simply continue it. Make a list of what you have to do for each project or paper. For example, if you have to write a research paper, chunk it down into steps like choosing a topic, writing an outline, researching the Net, going to the library, writing the first draft and so on. Once you know all the steps, you can put them where they belong on the list. Do this for each class and anything else that might require daily attention.

Your list might look like this:

MONDAY

Get books on Plato from the library.

Run one mile for track. Time it.

Study for tomorrow's literature quiz.

Get to lab for biology.

Science class from 10-12

TUESDAY

English class from 2-4

Work from 6-8

Write English outline on Plato

Meet with Dan and Kevin at 9

Call Mom and ask for more money

A list like this will help ensure that you don't waste time. You won't spend time wondering what you are supposed to do next or have to stop and look it up again. These lists will also work wonderfully with your day planner. While it has overall due dates, your list will have things broken down into steps. Can you guess the most important part about a list? Put it where you can see it, whether pinned to your bulletin board or inserted in your day planner. Just choose a place that you look at daily. Update it daily as well. When you have accomplished

---

What You Eat Counts

"If a freshman puts on 15 extra pounds from drinking beer alone, then that is a problem. But even if the extra weight comes from a mixture of beer and junk food, or junk food alone, I would urge you to do your best not to fall victim to this rite of passage. In the first place, it shows a lack of maturity—that without Mom constantly looking over your shoulder, you can't keep yourself from gorging on pizza and chips. It also means that you're probably not eating right, as I doubt that you're piling on the broccoli and carrots too. (It's not uncommon for college students to get diseases that come from not eating a proper diet and that are usually found only among the very poor who can't afford to eat the right foods.) Such extra weight may also indicate that you're not getting enough exercise. And, finally, it might start you on a lifetime of food problems, and that's definitely not one of the lessons you want to include in your college education."

— Dr. Ruth Westheimer, *Dr. Ruth's Guide to College Life*

something, check it off your list. Watch for the thrill as you achieve the items on your list. You will also know if you have missed something and have to add it to the next day's list.

(5) The basic elements of life.

Whether you are rushing to complete an assignment, make it to work on time or squeeze in an unexpected track practice, it's easy to over-look two simple things: sleeping and eating. You cut out a little sleep here, skip a meal or two there. It isn't much—but it builds up. The student who doesn't get enough sleep and food may accomplish more, but in the end, it will all fall apart and you will lose more time than you gain. (Advice on the inevitable but occasional all-nighter can be found in Chapter Eight.) You will be tired, cranky and more susceptible to get-ting sick. Take time to eat well and sleep at least seven hours a night or everything you gained by skipping both will be lost when you are exhausted or ill.

Here are two examples of what can happen with eating when you go to college. They may seem to be on opposite ends of the spectrum, but they really are quite similar because they both deal with food and control.

The first problem is one that faces a growing number of young people today: anorexia and bulimia. These eating disorders happen when the number of calories plummets due to limited or restricted eating, while physical activity increases. It may start out as just skipping a few meals to spend that time doing something else, but before you know, it can turn into a potentially fatal condition. If you find yourself missing meals on purpose and your weight dropping significantly, especially if this is accompanied with any signs of depression or anxiety, it's time to talk to someone. Get to the health center, talk to a friend or call home.

On the other hand, you might experience what is sometimes called "The Freshman 15." According to Roberta Anding, a spokesperson of the American Dietetic Association, about 60 percent of college students gain five to 25 pounds during their first year of school. It goes back to that "my parents aren't looking" philosophy. You can order pizza every night and don't have to get any fruits or vegetables as you go through the cafeteria line. You get to make the decision about what you are and are not going to eat. Ah! The power! Ah, the scales!

To avoid either of these two extremes, try these simple steps:

- Keep healthy snacks in your dorm room

- Eat your heaviest meals in the first part of the day, not the last

- Carry healthy snacks in your purse or backpack

- Avoid the sugary, carb-laden foods when you finally do eat

- Do not skip meals; at least have some fruit, a granola bar or something

For more suggestions, check out the Healing Well website at http://healingwell.healthology.com.

(6) The best time...

You have been trying to convince your parents for years that you study best late at night, right? You've launched multiple campaigns to get them to let you stay up really late and now is your chance to do it all the time. Finally you are in a place and situation where you can find out if that is true or not. Don't just assume you were right. Experiment a little. Study at night, in the morning and in the middle of the afternoon. Which seems to be the most effective? When are you most alert and receptive to information? You need to find what works best for you (And if it turns out to be early morning like your parents told you, we promise not to tell.).

(7) ...and place.

While you were trying to convince your parents that you study best after midnight, you might have also been telling them that you did it best in your room with music on loud, or even a few friends around. Once again, it's time to put that theory to the test.

Conduct a few experiments. Study in your room, at the library, in the lounge, at a friend's house or in the fraternity or sorority house. Study in silence or surrounded by music, people or television. Study on the bed, in a soft chair or a hard chair. Sit at a desk or lie on your bed. Try bright lights and dim lights. Even the type of music you listen to can have an influence. Try classical, country, gospel, opera, rock, blues, jazz, oldies, Broadway soundtracks. What seems to work best for you? Where does the material soak in the best? What is distracting and what is not? For some students, trying to read material and understand it in complete silence is a treat; for others, it is torture. Simple sounds like water dripping, clocks ticking or phones ringing can drive some people crazy, and others will not even notice them. Once you have found what works for you, stick with it.

Be sure to avoid internal distractions as well. Your ability to study can be compromised by simple things like being hungry, tired or sick. Extreme worry, boredom or even a drive for perfectionism can interfere with being able to concentrate. If you become aware of any of these factors, they need to be addressed, just as much as time and location do.

(8) And in your spare time...

Not that you have much of it, mind you...but what you do have should be used wisely. There are so many options to choose from and as you have found out already, there are only a few hours to give. Here is just a short list:

- sports

- clubs and organizations

- study groups

- part-time jobs

- meet with friends

- party

- volunteer work

What will bring you the most fulfillment? It's vital that you balance the fun with the work (see Chapter Eight). Too much of one or the other makes you a cranky student. Too much fun means that you're falling down in the academic department; not enough means you will end up stressed and burned out.

(9) Where does work fit in?

Should you work while you are in college? For many students, that isn't an option. They have to work to make ends meet for books, supplies and other costs not covered by scholarships, grants and parents. If it is an option, however, give it some serious thought. As you saw earlier in the chapter, time is of the essence right now, and work will definitely take up a lot of your time and energy.

In 2002, a report entitled "At What Cost?" was issued by the Public Interest Research Group Higher Education Project (www. pirg.org). It looked at how employment affected college students. Here is what the report found:

■ 74 percent of full-time students work while attending school

■ Of those, 84 percent identify themselves as primarily working to meet college expenses

■ 46 percent of full-time working students work 25 or more hours a week

■ 42 percent of these students reported that working hurt their grades

■ 53 percent of full-time working students who work 25 or more hours a week reported that employment limited their class schedule and 38 percent said that work limited their class choice

■ 63 percent of full-time working students who work 25 or more hours a week reported that they would not be able to afford college if they did not work

■ One in five full-time working students works 35 or more hours a week

As you can see, working may be essential to college survival, but it comes at a high price. Before you just accept the fact that you will have to work in college, do your scholarship/loan/grant homework. Start with Gen and Kelly Tanabe's book *Sallie Mae How to Pay for College*. It can give you a lot of information on finding ways to pay for college other than working in your every spare moment.

If you do have to work, see if you can find something that will give you added experience in your field of study. If you're studying animal medicine, work at a veterinarian's office, for example. Another option is work-study, which you may be offered as part of your financial aid package. The benefits of work-study are that your job will most likely be conveniently located on campus and your employer will be able to better work around your schedule. Also, be sure to put your schedule into your day planner and on your daily list. You will have to pay extra attention to sleeping enough and eating well because you will need everything you can get to keep up with all your demands.

(10) The most effective piece of equipment you will ever purchase.

Any guesses? Is it the perfect day planner? The toughest backpack? Maybe even the most high-tech computer? Good guesses, but the actual answer is (drum roll, please) a quality alarm lock. Being up on time is essential to getting to class and getting each day started the right way, so get a good one. Make sure it rings loudly and that you place it far away enough from your bed that you have to get up to turn it off. Never hit the snooze button. It's dangerous and addictive.

Remember that while time management may sound like a pain, you will get used to it. After you do, the results will be less stress and more efficiency and time to learn and play.

CHAPTER EIGHT

. . . .

Am I Having Fun Yet? The Top Ten of Balancing Social and Studies

A philosopher once said (ok, this is a bit paraphrased), "Virtue comes from following a course of action somewhere between the extreme of too much and that of too little." Another way to put it is "all things in moderation." Or simply, balance.

(1) Learn in groups.

By putting together a study group, you can blend two things at once: seeing your friends and getting your studying done. It is much easier to understand material if you have others who are learning the same thing. You can bounce questions off one another and if one of you grasps a certain concept first, he/she can explain it to the others in a way that might make more sense to them.

If you decide to organize a study group, keep a few things in mind:

- Always select people who have the same goal as you—and that doesn't mean how much pizza you can eat while cramming for a math test. You want to choose people who want to learn this information to do well in class.

- Look around your class and see which students seem to really be paying attention, taking notes, asking questions and responding to the professor. They are the ones you want to ask to be part of your study group.

- Most groups work best if there are more than three and less than seven. Too many of you and it turns from studying to partying.

College Students and Stress

Dr. Gregory Hall, Bentley College

Mind and body are integrated as can be seen with the issue of stress. It is no secret that psychological stress and physical illness are related. Stress triggers physiological and chemical (hormones) changes in the body. Physical illness is commonly accompanied with increased stress. Thus, as we learn to manage stress we must address physical as well as psychological factors. As you consider the following tips, keep in mind that maintaining balance between your intellectual, social and personal development is the key to a well-adjusted college experience.

■ Add a physical workout to your schedule at least every other day. One does not need to be gifted athletically to accomplish this. You can jog, power walk, use stepper, rowing or biking machines, swim or any other form of exercise. Do not see this as "recreational time" that can be blown off. Physical activity is a great way to insure that life's minor stresses do not build.

■ Set both long-term (this semester or this year) and short-term (this day or this week) goals. Write them down. Make them part of your time-management schedule.

■ Manage your time. Develop a schedule that provides for academic, social and physical time. Follow the schedule! Seek the help of an adviser in developing better time-management skills.

■ Each day find 20 minutes of "alone time" to relax. Take a walk, write in a journal or meditate.

■ Don't sweat the small stuff...always ask yourself if the issue at hand is worth getting upset about. If it isn't affecting your goal achievement, it may not be worth fretting over.

■ Humor and positive thinking are important tools in stress management.

■ Most importantly, communicate! Talking to a person who you trust be they a friend, roommate, family member, professor, significant other or co-worker about issues of concern is helpful. We all need someone to listen.

Reprinted with permission of CampusBlues.com.

When you are in your groups, use your time efficiently. Quiz one another over the material you've been working on. Ask questions if you don't understand something. Often the best teacher is another student.

(2) Choose wisely, young student.

You may well be overwhelmed with social opportunities at school. There are meetings for everyone, regardless of their interests or hobbies. There are often hundreds of classmates to meet and spend time with. There are sports to get involved in and sororities/fraternities to join. Your biggest complication will be making sure you do all these extracurricular activities in moderation. Before you commit to anything, get that day planner back out and make sure you really have time for it. Social life in college is very important, but it is not the primary reason you are there.

(3) Dating and sex.

If you think about the social aspects of college, dating certainly is one of the first issues to come up. Most likely, you will be dating during your college years. In fact, many students meet their future spouses during college. Advice about dating and sexuality is not within the scope of this book, except to say that both of them take time and you will have to balance that with your studies as well.

For some great advice on sexuality and the college student, check out the websites www.smartersex.org and teensexuality.studentcenter. org.

(4) Ignoring temptation.

Along with the many new educational and social opportunities that can come your way with college, there are also temptations. Certainly drugs is one of them. You may be sick of hearing "Just say no," so instead just say you've got too many other things to do with your time (and money!) than spend them on drugs. They are expensive, dangerous and carry the potential to destroy everything you have been working so hard for all these years. Common physical changes from drug use include lack of physical coordination (forget sports), puffy face, running nose, hacking cough and excessive sweating (forget dating) and hyperactivity and tremors (forget sitting in class). Behavioral changes are often worse, including moodiness, nervousness, lack of concentration and depression. Doesn't sound like much fun—why risk it?

You can find some terrific info on the Net about the nasty effects of drug use. The National Mental Health Association's website has some good data at www.nimh.nih.gov/publicat/students.cfm. So does a user-friendly site called Facts on Tap (www.factsontap.org). Check 'em out.

(5) It's just a few drinks...

Alcohol carries just as many dangers as drugs—perhaps even more since it is often easier and cheaper to get. Any "decent" party on campus features non-stop beer, right? Well, before you start thinking about all those great partying weekends ahead of you, keep in mind that according to a Harvard study, 31 percent of college students "meet the clinical criteria for alcohol abuse" (Harvard School of Public Health College Alcohol Study (CAS) www.hsph.harvard.edu/cas). According to the "Alcohol Policies Report" from the Center for Science in the Public Interest, college presidents believe that binge drinking is the most serious problem on campus. (Source: www.cspinet.org/booze/collfact1.htm) They also stated that frequent binge drinkers are 21 times more likely to miss class, fall behind in school work, get hurt and get in trouble with campus police.

In "A Call to Action: Changing the Culture of Drinking at U.S. Colleges" (written by the College Task Force of the National Advisory Council of Alcohol Abuse and Alcoholism), statistics include:

- 1,400 college students die each year from alcohol-related injuries

- 500,000 college students were injured under the influence of alcohol

- 600,000 college students are assaulted by students who have been drinking

- 70,000 college students are victims of alcohol-related sexual assault

- 150,000 college students develop an alcohol-related health problem

Are beer and hard liquor really worth all this? If you are convinced that drinking really is a part of college life, at least use some common sense and be, here's that word again, responsible.

(6) It can be all Greek to you—or not.

A great many colleges offer the chance to join on-campus sororities and fraternities. Whether or not you choose to join one is completely up to you and your personality. Just be aware that if you do, membership will require time. Get out the day planner!

From the outside looking in, the Greek life may look perfect. And while many people cherish the time they once spent in a fraternity or sorority there are aspects of it you should be aware of before you make your final decision.

First, there is the time involved. You are making a commitment to participate in activities including rush, community service and social events.

Second, there is money involved. If you are on a tight budget, you should know that membership can range from $100 to $900 per semester.

Don't get me wrong. Becoming part of a campus' Greek life can be delightful. If you want to meet more people and have more friends, this is one good way to do it. Membership in a sorority or fraternity can teach you some great lessons in leadership, socializing and teamwork.

(7) Dorm life can be fun!

Years from now, when you look back at your college experience, you will most likely sigh wistfully, remembering wonderful times you had in your dorm room. While some students may live in off-campus housing, the majority will be in a dorm on campus. Some colleges require you live in a dorm for at least the first year. You will make some great friends, learn how to live with and get along with others and hopefully like your roommate.

Dorms often have activities, from television marathons to singing contests to slumber parties. If you take the time to join in now and then, you will find that you suddenly not only know a lot more people on campus, but they are also living so close to you that getting together is nooooooo problem. As the people at www.collegeboard.com say, "The dorms can help jump start your social life, ease the transition to life on your own and introduce you to a diverse group of people. Sure, living in a dorm can have its drawbacks—no privacy, crowded bathrooms, weird roommates. But most people find that the rewards outweigh the frustrations."

(8) I'm feeling pretty low.

College is exciting, fun, demanding—and stressful. It's easy to feel overwhelmed by everything from the increased academic demands, being in a new environment and the financial responsibilities to the shift in your social life and exposure to new people and possibilities. Depression can set in almost before you realize it. It comes out differently in each person. Some are always irritated, others cry and others never say a word.

According to the National Institute for Mental Health, here are the major symptoms of depression:

- Sadness, anxiety or "empty" feelings

- Decreased energy, fatigue, being "slowed down"

- Loss of interest or pleasure in usual activities

- Sleep disturbances (insomnia, oversleeping or waking much earlier than usual)

- Appetite and weight changes (either loss or gain)

- Feelings of hopelessness, guilt and worthlessness

- Thoughts of death or suicide or suicide attempts

- Difficulty concentrating, making decisions or remembering things

- Irritability or excessive crying

- Chronic aches and pains not explained by another physical condition

A less intense type of depression, dysthymia, involves long-term, chronic symptoms that are less severe but keep you from functioning at your full ability and from feeling well.

In bipolar illness (also known as manic-depressive illness), cycles of depression alternate with cycles of elation and increased activity, known as mania.

What can be done if you find you are suffering from some or all of these symptoms? Just recognizing them is a good first step. Next, find someone to talk to about what you are experiencing. Don't ignore it. Speak with your residential assistant or in more serious cases seek professional help.

(9) Same day, different people.

One of college's biggest perks is that it introduces you to the wide world of diversity. If you grew up in a small town, this will be especially evident. You will most likely be surrounded by students from all ethnic groups, from whites and African-Americans to Hispanic to Asian and Native American. There will be international students from countries around the world. You will meet gays, lesbians and bisexuals. Some students will have come from poor backgrounds, others from wealthy. The small-town students will sit right next to the students from New York City or Chicago. This is a wonderful opportunity for you to learn about other people and find out how different—and how alike—they all are. Don't waste it.

(10) Pulling the inevitable all-nighter.

Chances are you will pull a number of all-nighters. Maybe you fell behind, maybe you need more time to understand a concept or 12, maybe you just found out about tomorrow's test, maybe it's mid-terms or

---

Advice on Sleep

If you're planning your class schedule before you actually arrive at college, be sure to leave some mornings free so that you can sleep late. You can only go so many days in a row on four or five hours' rest.

Pack some earplugs. There will be nights when you're utterly exhausted and will need to conk out before dawn. Remember, sleep deprivation has been used as a form of torture, so don't suffer needlessly.

Cat naps can be quite refreshing. Even 15 minutes' worth of sleep in between classes can keep you going.

Don't abuse caffeine, in whatever form. You need to sleep to absorb what you are studying, so staying up all night before an exam will only have a negative impact.

If you really are having problems staying awake in class, go to see your RA. This is one roommate problem where there is the potential for help. If others in your dorm report having the same problem, then you can switch roommates so that you share quarters with someone who also likes to get to sleep at a reasonable hour.

— Dr. Ruth Westheimer, *Dr. Ruth's Guide to College Life*

finals week or maybe you just want to study more than you usually do. Whatever the reason, if you are going to do it, do it right.

First of all, have food and drink nearby. You will need it to keep up your strength and provide some necessary energy. Have something in your room and take regular breaks to snack. As much as you would like to stock up on lattes and M and M's, you will be better off with some fruit and juice or water. Too much caffeine and/or sugar will just make you jittery instead of energetic.

Choose a place to study that is not terribly comfortable. Make the chair harder than you prefer, keep it cool in the room and don't grab any pillows or blankets. Keep far, far away from soft chairs, couches or beds. You may think you're just pausing for a rest but the next thing you know, it is 9 a.m. and you didn't get near the studying done that you needed.

Give yourself incentives. When you finish a chapter, you will have a snack, call a friend, take a quick shower or whatever would be rewarding for you.

As odd as it sounds, try to have fun with an all-nighter. When you were in high school, the idea of staying up all night like this would have been exciting. Enjoy it. Listen to your favorite music and just relish the moment. You might not have this chance again for years.

If you can arrange it, pull your all-nighter with a friend ... or six. If you are all studying for the same test, you can quiz each other. Just having other friends with you will automatically make it more fun and help keep you awake.

Keep in mind that all-nighters are occasional events. They should never be depended on for keeping up on your classes. They are a measure of last resort because too many of them will turn you into an exhausted student, not a successful one.

CHAPTER NINE
. . . .

Where's Mom When I Need Her? The Top Ten of Living on Your Own

Living on your own is wonderful, exhilarating, empowering and ... often a lot more work than you had ever anticipated. You will most likely be utterly amazed at how much your mom, dad or other guardian did on a daily basis for you that you never really noticed. It will become quite evident when those services suddenly disappear and you have to give thought to bizarre things like getting the toothpaste you like most or fixing buttons that fell off your shirt.

If you live in the dorm, some of life's basics are taken care of. You don't have to worry about paying the electricity, heat or water bills like you might if you live off campus (unless you're renting and then that is often the landlord's headache, not yours.) No matter where you live, however, you may be easily overwhelmed at what you have to take care of beyond just going to class and keeping up with your studies.

The best piece of advice when it comes to living on your own is start practicing while you are still at home and can falter with fewer consequences. Ask someone to show you how to properly do laundry. Learn to cook some simple meals. Talk to a parent about how to budget money. Find out where you can find that special flavor of toothpaste or your favorite shampoo. (Perhaps you already know all this! In that case, congratulations. When you get to college, you might be able to teach your dorm mates a thing or two.)

In case you don't know already or aren't planning to learn before you get to college, here is a list of some basics you will need to make this powerful position of living alone a little easier.

(1) Smart laundry.

Laundry will be one of the most important life skills you need. If you are going to community college or head home every weekend, you might be able to avoid this chore for a while. But face it, one day you really will have to do this without help, so why not start now when your learning curve is at its peak?

Hopefully you have spent your life not dividing things into black and white (including everything from people to what to report on your tax returns). However, this is one time where you can throw out that rule. Divide your clothes into dark and light before washing them. (At what point you decide something is officially "dirty" is up to you. Chances are, it will be much later than what your mother would have liked and just before it can stand up on its own in your closet.)

Most clothes are easy to separate, but what about that black and white shirt or the red and pink skirt? Go with darks and hope for the best.

Before laundering anything, check the label in the clothes. You might have something that requires special handling, like that delicate sweater with the beading on it. You might also have clothing that is dry cleaning only. These will take extra effort, either to put together enough for a delicate load in the washer or a trip to the closest dry cleaner.

Once it is time to hit the dorm's laundry room or the college's laundromat, keep the following rules in mind:

- Have lots and lots of quarters on hand.

- Check the pockets of everything you wash to make sure they don't contain money, tickets, tissues or anything else that could be damaged.

- Don't overload the washer or the dryer.

- Fold the clothes when they come out of the dryer and you won't have to iron them as much (if at all) later. If you're asking what's an iron, then just don't worry about it. You're used to wrinkles by now.

If you think that doing laundry is so awful that it belongs on one

> Laundry is sorted into two piles. Dirty and Offensive. Dirty may be worn again. Offensive must be washed. Learn the compost method of cleaning in which the heat and weight from the top of the pile cleans the clothes on the bottom of the pile.
>
> —Youth minister Steve Case at Windermere Union United Church of Christ, excerpt from www. youthspecialities.com

level of Dante's version of hell, consider asking someone else to do it for you. You could barter—you will help them with math class for an hour for each load done, or you could just pay them.

(2) Beating the health inspector.

If health inspectors came to dorm rooms, colleges and universities across the country would be shut down for multiple violations. Keeping a dorm room clean seems simple. After all, it's not very big and there are only one or two of you in there most of the time. So how does it manage to look like a hurricane went through anyway? Just consider it a talent.

Keeping your dorm room clean doesn't mean it has to look like your house back home did. You probably don't have the time, energy or interest in keeping it that clean. Some simple tricks can help though. Try these:

- Put up a bulletin board to hold all your important papers so they aren't all over the place.

- Make your bed every morning before you do anything else. It sounds like a drag, but you will be surprised at what a difference it makes. In such a small room, your bed often serves as the place to sleep, eat, rest, study, talk and relax. If it's all rumpled up, you will be less likely to use it. To simplify making it, have a large comforter instead of bedspread so you can just take hold of everything and yank, smooth and you're finished. While keeping tons of things on your bed may seem like a good idea at first, you may find yourself whittling it down as days go by and you have to move it every night and replace it all every morning.

- Dust around things once a month, unless company is coming. If it's your parents, pick everything up and dust carefully. Wait for them to mutter to each other about how much you have matured since you left for college.

- Set up a special place to keep your backpack and/or purse. Always put it there and it won't get lost in the daily shuffle.

- If you have a sink in your room, clean it at least once a week. There are disinfecting wipes that just require a quick wipe-down. If not, be prepared for rainbow-colored growths, something that is not only unsightly but also can make you sick.

(3) Ya Gotta Eat!

Perhaps one of the biggest complaints about adjusting to college life is the food. Most students eat in the cafeteria, and while some are pretty darn good, others aren't. Here are a few suggestions for dealing with not getting your favorite meals anymore.

- Keep some food in your dorm room. A small fridge is a great thing to ask for when your grandparents want to get you something for your room.

- Be open minded to new foods. Don't turn your nose up and keep being picky (That's what little kids do, not big, tough college students.).

- Eat out now and again, as long as you keep within your budget and don't overdo it.

- Order out pizza occasionally, but watch out for those Freshman 15.

- Go grocery shopping and keep actual meal food in your room rather than just snacks.

- Learn some basic cooking skills. Many dorms have small kitchens where you can prepare your own meals. How tough is a microwavable pot pie anyway?

(4) What's a budget again?

Whether you are paying for college with your parent's money, a scholarship, working or a combination of all three, you will need to learn how to budget. This will come in mighty handy when you are living on your own after school too.

A budget should be firm but not inflexible. Life always presents a few surprises along the way that will require you to adjust where your money is going, but you still should have a standard plan to follow.

Budgeting is not that complicated a process. It is a matter of making a list of your expenses and income and finding a balance between the two.

When you look at your expenses, figure how much you will need for:

- tuition

- rent/room and board

- car payments

- car insurance

- parking fees

- utilities

- entertainment

- gasoline

- food

- hygiene stuff

- clothing

- car repair

- books

- phone bills

- dating

The first five are usually preset amounts and absolutely due on time. They are considered "fixed" costs. The others are "variable," meaning the lifestyle choices you make can affect the amounts. If you cut back on eating out, going to movies and other entertainment, that expense is quickly reduced. You can do a lot to affect those numbers just by making decisions to do so. It takes discipline but is possible. After all, your parents have been doing it for years!

The next thing you do is look at what money you have coming in. This can come from:

- parents

- grants

- scholarships

- loans

- jobs

Those were the easy steps. Now for the more difficult part: comparing the two. It doesn't take a math major to figure out that if your monthly expenses are running more than your income, something has to change. This is where you go back to your list of variable expenses and start paring them down as much as possible to get those two numbers a lot closer together. If you get stuck, give your parents a call. No, not to get more money but to ask for budgeting advice.

(5) I'm out of everything. Where do I get dental floss?

Before you leave home, make a list of the hygiene supplies you like the best. Take the list and do one of two things: Give it to your parents and have them buy a dozen of each so you don't have to face running out for a long time or find out where each product can be purchased and keep the list in your dorm's desk drawer for quick and easy referencing. Things you might want to include are: soap, perfume/cologne, deodorant, toothpaste, dental floss, makeup, lotions, shaving cream and razors. Of course, a third option is to send the list to your grandparents or favorite aunt or uncle and hope they take pity and send you keeping clean care packages.

Beware of Credit Cards

Special warning: Despite the incredibly cutesy commercials credit card companies keep putting on the television and in magazines and the offers of free T-shirts on campus, credit cards are not the solution to running low on money. Credit cards (which deservedly should be referred to as debt cards since that's what happens to a lot of people when they rely on those handy pieces of plastic) are risky for most people. For young adults newly on their own, they can be poison. With interest rates that are often double and triple regular rates and stiff penalties for spending over the limit or late payments, your small purchases can turn into a giant problem. Credit cards should be used for unexpected emergencies and primarily with parental permission. You have years ahead of you to struggle with dealing with the chronic seduction of credit cards; don't start now.

(6) Learning to do without.

While you may have used two cars and a U-Haul to move all your stuff to college, most students don't. They pack what they can fit in one car and settle for that. The luxuries you had at home are just not going to be available at college. For instance, while many students bring their own computers with them, some are not able to. In that case, check how to get access to one. It can be your roommate's (with permission, of course!), a college computer, the ones at the library, whatever you can find.

Other luxuries that you once took for granted while living at home but now may miss desperately are a stereo, refrigerator and television. There are several solutions to this. Hope your roommate has one and is generous, try to pick one up at a local thrift store, start making your Christmas lists now and put aside money any chance you get until you can afford one. There is one more—get used to not having them. Just think how much you will appreciate them again once you get back home for holidays or weekends.

(7) Dad, where do I put the oil?

If you are going to have a car at college, learn some simple repairs. Start with the very basics like changing a flat tire, changing the oil and checking the battery. They are easy to do and can be unbelievably convenient in important moments.

You can get the information from several sources. There are tons of books on car care, from simple to advanced mechanics. You can also try asking someone in your family to show you or take a shop class in high school that will teach what you need to know.

(8) I feel crummy.

The first time you feel sick at college can feel mighty lonely. Maybe you miss the chicken soup your older sister would make for you or the way your mom feels your forehead to monitor your temperature. Just remember that most every college has its own infirmary or health center, so use it. They are there to give you confidential and competent help. Friends can help you keep up on what you are missing in class and run to the store to get you another bottle of your favorite soda. If worse comes to worst, call home and get unconditional sympathy.

(9) Late night stroll...or not.

Everyone has watched a scary movie where the plucky heroine takes off into the dark, dank, dreary basement of a house, armed with nothing other than a wavering candle, right? You shout at the television screen, "You idiot! At least take a flashlight so you can hit someone over the head with it. What are you thinking going there all alone? You know better!" You can guarantee that if you head out across campus alone at night, someone will be shouting the same thing at you. College life is wonderful, but it has its problems, and crime on campus is one of them. Don't complicate your life by putting yourself at risk unnecessarily. Finals are stressful enough; you don't need to add staying safe to your list of things to worry about.

Here are some important rules to keep in mind about campus safety. Heed them well. Hint: This is a good one to make a copy of and pin up on your wall.

DORM SAFETY

■ Don't let anyone into the dorm that you don't personally know. (This goes for pizza deliverymen too!)

■ Keep your dorm room door locked all through the night and whenever you are gone. If you leave to go to the laundry room, bathroom or another friend's dorm room, lock your door behind you.

■ Never, ever lend your dorm room key to anyone.

PARKING LOT SAFETY

■ Keep your car locked at all times.

■ Don't keep your valuables out where someone can see them. Put them in your trunk, under the seats or bring them into your room with you.

■ Never walk out to your car alone at night. Have someone go with you, even if it is your campus' escort service.

■ Have your keys ready in your hand as you approach the car.

■ Check the back seat before getting into the car.

PERSONAL SAFETY

- Never walk alone—especially at night. Remember the girl in the horror movie? You're smarter than that!

- Walk only in well-lit areas, not dark alleys or shortcuts.

- Trust your instincts. If you feel a place or situation is dangerous, you just may be right. Play it safe and go to a populated area or call campus security on your cell phone.

- Find out where all campus emergency phones are located.

PARTY SAFETY

- Don't go to a party alone.

- Drink responsibly.

- Always tell your friends where you are going.

- Take a cell phone with you.

- Have the number of a local taxi service and/or the campus bus service on you at all times.

DATING SAFETY

- Find out who your date is. Google him/her!

- Know his/her first and last name and address. Where does he/she go to school? Where does he/she work?

- Tell your friends exactly who you are going with and where you are going.

- Set up a time to check in and if you don't, your friends should call for help.

- Carry a cell phone at all times.

- Stay in public places on your date.

- Have a way to get home should the date not quite go as well as you hoped.

Keep in mind that while these precautions may seem a little paranoid, they are important. In 1986, a freshman named Jeanne Clery was sleeping in her dorm room at Lehigh University. She was murdered there and her parents discovered that the campus had not told anyone about the 38 violent crimes that had already occurred on the campus. They helped pass the Jeanne Clery Disclosure of Campus Security Policy and Campus Crime Statistics Act. It is a federal law that requires colleges and universities across the country to disclose information about crimes on and around their campuses. This law is enforced by the U.S. Department of Education. It requires:

■ Schools must publish an annual report disclosing campus security policies and three years' worth of selected crime statistics.

■ Schools must make timely warnings to the campus community about crimes that pose an ongoing threat to students and employees.

■ Each institution with a police or security department must have a public crime log.

■ The U.S. Department of Education centrally collects and disseminates the crime statistics.

■ Campus sexual assault victims are assured of certain basic rights.

■ Schools that fail to comply can be fined by the DOE.

Source: www.securityoncampus.org

(10) How am I supposed to get there?

One of the biggest things students tend to miss when they get to college is transportation. Mom and Dad (and their respective cars) are no longer available. Many colleges will not allow first-year students to have their own cars on campus. So how do you get from one place to another? Well, the first obvious choice for campus travel is your feet. You will probably never do as much walking in your life as you do that first year of college. (That's good though. It will help work off those extra pounds from all the pizza!) Spend some big bucks on comfy walking shoes. They will become your new best friends.

A bicycle is a great way to get places faster and get exercise to boot. Invest in a good bike lock to keep it safe and sound.

If you want to go off campus, check into local buses. They often run near the campus to help students get where they need to go. You might also talk to other students with cars to see about carpooling into the city.

Being on your own is wonderful. You will be amazed at how fast your life changes and how you learn to accept responsibilities that you had never thought about before. The key is being prepared so that you don't have to recover from shock before you can start learning. Don't wait. Get as many skills as you can now and you will be relieved later.

SECTION 5

THE COLLEGES

A Guide to the Colleges that Welcome B Students

A Guide to the Colleges that Welcome B Students

As a B or C student, you have many options when it comes to finding a college that is right for you. In fact, there are far more colleges that want you than you could ever apply to in a single year. Your challenge will not be finding the right college but narrowing down your list of possibilities.

As you will see, not all colleges require certain GPAs or test scores to make it past the velvet rope. Now it's time to meet some of the schools that not only accept B and C students but that also embrace them. These colleges are competitive and offer the highest quality educations, but they also recognize that students like you have much to offer and are committed to ensuring your success.

How These Colleges Were Chosen

All of the colleges and universities were chosen for several reasons.

■ **They each offer very high quality educations.** Just because they accept students with less-than-perfect scores doesn't mean that they sacrifice quality. These schools are committed to preparing you for your future.

■ **B and C students are welcome.** These colleges have test score and GPA averages that fit well with the typical B student's range. In addition, they offer programs such as tutoring or mentoring that will help students like you succeed once you are in college.

■ **They are competitive.** While not as selective as many of the colleges at the top of news magazines' lists, they do have standards for admission. Because they generally draw from a smaller geographic area, community colleges are not included.

■ **They offer diversity.** These schools represent all parts of the country and all sizes, from small to large.

The Profiles

The college profiles have the essential information you need to determine if the school is a good fit for you academically, financially and career-wise. Here are some important definitions to help you make the most of the profiles:

Percentage of applicants admitted: This statistic gives a general sense of the level of competitiveness of the college and represents the undergraduate admission rate.

Average GPA range: This is the average high school GPA of admitted undergraduates.

SAT/ACT range: These represent the range between the 25th and 75th percentile of scores of accepted undergraduate students, or the middle 50 percent. In other words, for a range of 500 to 600 on the math SAT exam, 25 percent of accepted students scored below 500, 25 percent scored above 600 and 50 percent scored between 500 and 600.

Number of undergraduates: Knowing this gives an indication of what the campus life will be like, as well as the size and scope of the school.

Costs: While it's useful to know the costs of tuition, fees, books and supplies and room and board, keep in mind that most students do not pay the full sticker price of a college. Financial aid and scholarships can bring the costs of college down.

Favorite majors: These are the five largest programs at the college.

The B features: These are the features offered by the colleges that can be especially helpful for students like you. Included are tutoring programs, the faculty-student ratio and programs to ease the transition from high school to college. You'll see the active role each college is taking in helping you succeed.

Featured profiles: Certain profiles are much longer than others. This is because at these schools, the admission department took time out to speak at length about their welcoming policies for B students.

Special Request: If you get in touch with any of the places here, be sure to tell them you found them here!

List of Colleges by Name

List of Colleges by Location

Maine

Maryland

Massachusetts

Michigan

Minnesota

Mississippi

Missouri

Wyoming

Adelphi University

Garden City, NY

Address: One South Avenue, Garden City, NY 11530
Phone: 1-800-ADELPHI or 516-877-3050
Admissions email: admissions@adelphi.edu
Admissions contact: Christine Murphy, director of admissions
Website: www.adelphi.edu

Admissions Stats

Percentage of applicants admitted: 70.2% of freshman applicants
Average GPA range: 3.3-3.4
SAT range: 500-600 verbal, 500-610 math
ACT range: 22-26 composite, 22-26 English, 20-26 math

Size

Number of undergraduates: 4,425

Cost

Tuition and fees: $19,720
Books and supplies: $1,000
On campus room and board and other expenses: $11,490
Off campus room and board and other expenses: $10,000

Academics

Favorite majors: education, business, social sciences, health professions, visual and performing arts, psychology

Student Life

The campus: Chartered in 1896, Adelphi was the first institution of higher education for the liberal arts and sciences on Long Island. Its main campus is in Garden City, New York, and it also has centers in Manhattan, Hauppauge and Poughkeepsie, New York. The campus covers 75 lush acres and has six residence halls. It is 45 minutes away from New York City.

The students: Undergraduate students come from 38 states and 45 foreign countries.

The B Features

Has offered a General Studies program since 1985. According to the university, it is designed for "motivated high school seniors who demonstrate the potential for academic success, but who have not met the traditional academic admission requirements. Counselors, faculty members and administrators identify potentially successful candidates on the basis of their applications and letters of recommendation, as well as through personal interviews." The program offers small classes and personal advisement for each student. At the end of the year, students who have met all of the requirements continue as sophomores in the school's other undergraduate programs.

Insight

"Our admissions process is holistic," says Esther Goodcuff, associate vice president for enrollment management and student affairs. "We carefully read every single piece of documentation in each application. Our General Studies program is not a remedial program but one that challenges students, while at the same time supports them. Our faculty does individual tutoring outside of class and students are given an academic counselor to help with college transition issues." Goodcuff says that Adelphi's admissions department looks at trends in how students have been performing in high school, watching for an upward movement. "Letters of recommendation and the essay also give us a sense of just who you are," she adds. "We look for students who are highly motivated and truly want to do well."

Student Perspective

Crispin Booker from Brooklyn, New York. He is majoring in computer management and information systems. A graduate of Lafayette High School, he was a member of the varsity basketball team during his junior and senior year. He managed to maintain a 3.0 average during his senior year when he was the captain of the team and participated in community service projects with the Key Club.

"My expectations were to attend a prestigious university, which would provide me with the tools and opportunities to compete in a tough job market and to make a difference in my life and others," he says. "Plus, I wanted to learn in a diverse academic environment that would allow me to share my experiences with those from other ethnic backgrounds. Adelphi University has met my expectations, giving me a sense of direction in my life. The rigorous course work from the General Studies program and the diversity among the professors and students has helped me to focus and excel. In addition, I believe the program has prepared me for a demanding job market. I was able to take several challenging courses such as math, psychology, history, philosophy and English.

"I ultimately chose Adelphi because of its proximity to home and the prestigious General Studies program," he explains. "I also enjoyed the fact that it's close to New York City and I would have more job opportunities coming out of a well-known university like Adelphi. My short-term goals are to complete my bachelor's in computer management and information systems or history. My career goals are to complete law school and become a corporate lawyer.

"The experiences with my classmates are ones to remember," he adds. "I've met all types of people during the program and made many friends due to the various group assignments. In addition to the assignments, we got a chance to network and bond since a majority of us have to complete the same work and we can help each other. My experiences with my professors result in a lasting friendship because we spend so much time together during tutoring and counseling sessions," he continues. "They have helped me start my college career in a positive way, especially by reviewing my papers. Plus, I've really connected with my professors because of the individual attention they provide.

"I have found that the most challenging part about college is time management because there are so many things to do on campus, and so many people to meet. I learned that it is beneficial to set aside study time so I won't fall behind in the General Studies program," says Booker.

"I like campus life because there are so many activities to participate in. I'm the vice president of the Adelphi chapter of NAACP and also participate in other minority-based organizations. In addition," he concludes, "I work two on-campus jobs, one in operations and the other security."

The New York Times describes Adelphi as "thriving" and Jay Matthews of *The Washington Post* says Adelphi is "one of 100 hidden higher education jewels."

Agnes Scott College *

Decatur, GA

Address: 141 E. College Way, Decatur, GA 30030-3797
Phone: 404-471-6285
Admissions email: admissions@agnesscott.edu
Website: www.agnesscott.edu

Admissions Stats

Percentage of applicants admitted: 59.2%
SAT range: 540-680 verbal, 500-620 math
ACT range: 22-28 composite

Size

Number of undergraduates: 898

Cost

Tuition and fees: $22,050
Books and supplies: $700
On campus room and board and other expenses: $9,100
Off campus room and board and other expenses: $3,400

Academics

Favorite majors: social sciences, biological and biomedical sciences, psychology, English language and literature/letters, visual and performing arts

---

The B Features

Besides being the setting for the horror flick *Scream 2*, Agnes Scott offers smaller classes (10-19), often with less than a half dozen students. The school offers "talking study halls," centers with tables and comfy chairs where students can gather to discuss homework assignments as a group. Every student is given an admission counselor who works with the student from beginning to end on the application process.

* All women college

Albertson College of Idaho

Caldwell, ID

Address: 2112 Cleveland Boulevard, Caldwell, ID 83605-4432
Phone: 208-459-5306
Admissions email: admissions@albertson.edu
Website: www.albertson.edu

Admissions Stats

Percentage of applicants admitted: 81.8%
SAT range: 520-640 verbal, 500-620 math
ACT range: 21-26 composite, 20-27 English, 20-26 math

Size

Number of undergraduates: 818

Cost

Tuition and fees: $15,080
Books and supplies: $800
On campus room and board and other expenses: $6,400
Off campus room and board and other expenses: $5,750

Academics

Favorite majors: biological and biomedical sciences, psychology, visual and performing arts, social sciences, business, management, marketing and related support services

The B Features

All freshmen at this college must go through the First Year Experience, which consists of three parts and is geared to help each student connect "personally, academically and socially with their peers and with the College." The first part is called the First Year Book and consists of assigning a specific book to be read and then campus events such as speakers, contests, movies and discussions are centered around it. This helps students have a common point to begin talking and making friends.

The second part is Student Mentor, which links first-year students with junior or senior student mentors. Their role is to help each new student get involved in campus activities and guide them to helpful resources.
The third part is First Year Advising in which several advisors are dedicated to helping first-year students transition from high school to college life.

Albion College

· ·

Albion, MI

Address: 611 E. Porter Street, Albion, MI 49224
Phone: 517-629-0321
Admissions email: admissions@albion.edu
Website: www.albion.edu

Admissions Stats

Percentage of applicants admitted: 85.8%
SAT range: 512-640 verbal, 520-660 math
ACT range: 22-27 composite, 21-28 English, 21-27 math

Size

Number of undergraduates: 525

Cost

Tuition and fees: $22,918
Books and supplies: $700
On campus room and board and other expenses: $7,236
Off campus room and board and other expenses: $7,236

Academics

Favorite majors: social sciences, psychology, biological and biomedical sciences, English language and literature/letters, business, management, marketing and related support services

---
The B Features

Albion wants its new students to transition well into college life and provides a First Year Experience, as others do. It offers Common Reading, followed up by presentations by the author, as well as a program called Student Orientation, Advising and Registration (SOAR). It takes place in May before your first year begins and is two days of touring the campus, meeting people, eating in the dining hall, speaking to faculty, planning your schedule and even registering for fall classes. The first three days of your first year center around fun get-acquainted activities such as skits, singing, lectures, ice cream breaks and even comedians.

Albion offers classes smaller than 20 students, and many undergrads speak highly of the casual and friendly attitudes of the entire faculty.

Alcorn State University

· ·

Alcorn State, MS

Address: 1000 ASU Drive, Alcorn State, MS 39096
Phone: 601-877-6147
Admissions email: admissions@lorman.alcorn.edu
Website: www.alcorn.edu

Admissions Stats

Percentage of applicants admitted: 35.2%
SAT range: A minimum score of 790 is required.
ACT range: 16-20 composite, 15-18 English, 15-18 math

Size

Number of undergraduates: 2,662

Costs

Tuition and fees: $3,732 in state, $8,463 out of state
Books and supplies: $1,320
On campus room and board and other expenses: $8,412
Off campus room and board and other expenses: $9,766

Academics

Favorite majors: liberal arts and sciences, general studies and humanities, business, management, marketing and related support services, health professions and related clinical services, education, biological and biomedical services

---

The B Features

This is primarily an African American college, although about 8 percent of the students are Caucasian or of other ethnic backgrounds. Classes are small, and College for Excellence is offered for all freshmen, returning and transfer students. This program plans, supervises and coordinates all academic experiences of these students. It has an advising and tutoring staff and state of the art computer labs to help. Professional advisors support students by helping them adjust to college life, teaching about Alcorn and its policies, exploring career options, solving any problems that come along, teaching good test taking and studying and time management skills and monitoring progress. Students who are having problems in reading, writing or thinking skills are assisted so that they can quickly reach college-level proficiency.

Alfred University

Alfred, NY

Address: One Saxon Drive, Alfred, NY 14802-1205
Phone: 607-871-2115
Admissions email: admwww@alfred.edu
Website: www.alfred.edu

Admissions Stats

Percentage of applicants admitted: 72.8%
SAT range: 500-610 verbal, 500-610 math
ACT range: 21-26 composite, 20-26 English, 20-26 math

Size

Number of undergraduates: 2,055

Costs

Tuition and fees: $20,060
Books and supplies: $800
On campus room and board and other expenses: $10,574
Off campus room and board and other expenses: $8,800

Academics

Favorite majors: visual and performing arts, engineering, business, management, marketing and related support services, psychology, communication, journalism and related programs

The B Features

Rumored to have been the inspiration for the 1980s sit-com *Northern Exposure*, this college is quiet and small but active. The school is especially known for its School of Engineering's glass and ceramic programs and is one of the few schools that offer a degree in Ceramic Engineering. Classes are typically less than 10 students at Alfred, and it typically appeals to the back-to-nature student who likes cold and snowy winters. Each applicant is considered individually and with true, personal attention.

Anna Maria College

Paxton, MA

Address: 10 Sunset Lane, Paxton, MA 01612
Phone: 508-849-3360
Admissions email: admissions@annamaria.edu
Website: www.annamaria.edu

Admissions Stats

Percentage of applicants admitted: 90.7%
SAT range: 400-510 verbal, 400-490 math
ACT range: 11-12 composite

Size

Number of undergraduates: 731

Costs

Tuition and fees: $20,335
Books and supplies: $800
On campus room and board and other expenses: $9,045
Off campus room and board and other expenses: $6,530

Academics

Favorite majors: security and protective services, business, management, marketing and related support services, health professions and related clinical services, liberal arts and sciences, general studies and humanities and public administration and social service professions

The B Features

This Roman Catholic-based college was founded by the Sisters of St. Anne. It offers Career Resources to all students who are struggling to decide on a profession, and workshops are offered in the classroom as well as on campus on such topics as writing a resume, searching for jobs and improving interview skills. In addition, the Counseling Center offers helpful programs and workshops on subjects such as stress management and conflict resolution.

Anna Maria's Learning Center provides free assistance to all students. Professional and student tutors help in areas such as math, science, business and history. Sessions are usually held once or twice a week per term. Handouts on topics such as note taking, test taking and time management are always available. Each semester, a series of study skills workshops are taught.

Arizona State University

Tempe, AZ

Address: P.O. Box 870112, Tempe, AZ 85287
Phone: 480-965-7788
Admissions email: askasu@asu.edu
Website: www.asu.edu

Admissions Stats

Percentage of applicants admitted: 86.1%
SAT range: 490-600 verbal, 500-620 math
ACT range: 21-26 composite, 19-26 English, 20-27 math

Size

Number of undergraduates: 38,627

Costs

Tuition and fees: $12,919 out of state, $4,064 in state
Books and supplies: $838
On campus room and board and other expenses: $10,300
Off campus room and board and other expenses: $10,300

Academics

Favorite majors: business, management, marketing and related support services, communication, journalism and related programs, multi/interdisciplinary studies, education and social sciences

The B Features

Like other colleges, ASU offers First Year Experience for freshmen. According to the college, this program is designed to "provide a strong foundation for all first-year students and students in transition that will foster their academic and personal success. We will achieve this mission by providing academic support services, opportunities for the exchange of ideas, workshops, generating and supporting research and scholarship, hosting visiting scholars and practitioners, faculty interaction within living and learning communities, administering a website and student involvement opportunities with the university community."

The Learning Resource Center offers tutoring to help students develop study skills and strategies. This nationally certified program offers tutoring in more than 100 courses, either in a group or individual setting. Peer Coaching teaches time management, study habits and test taking skills. It also has software training and Academic Skills Workshops.

Auburn University

· ·

Auburn, AL

Address: Office of Undergraduate Recruiting and University Scholarships, The Quad Center, Auburn University, AL 36849
Phone: 334-844-4080
Admissions email: admissions@main.auburn.edu
Website: www.auburn.edu

Admissions Stats

Percentage of applicants admitted: 84.2%
SAT range: 500-600 verbal, 520-610 math
ACT range: 22-27 composite, 21-28 English, 20-26 math

Size

Number of undergraduates: 19,251

Costs

Tuition and fees: $14,048 out of state, $4,828 in state
Books and supplies: $900
On campus room and board and other expenses: $8,647
Off campus room and board and other expenses: $9,116

Academics

Favorite majors: business, management, marketing and related support services, social sciences, engineering, education, health professions and related clinical sciences

The B Features

Auburn has a network of academic advisors by department of major. Advisors assist students with selecting classes, career planning and general advice. Some also provide information about the department to prospective applicants.

Learning Communities bring together first-year students in the same major to take certain required classes as a group. This enables students to easily form study groups and to navigate classes cooperatively.

Departments also offer help for their students. For example, the Auburn Office of Engineering Student Services offers help to freshmen and transfer engineering students who need assistance in entry-level math, chemistry and physics classes. The tutoring is provided by volunteer upperclassmen who are doing well in those subjects and is either through group or one on one learning.

Augsburg College

Minneapolis, MN

Address: 2211 Riverside Avenue, Minneapolis, MN 55454
Phone: 612-330-1001
Admissions email: admissions@augsburg.edu
Admissions contact: Bethany Bierman, assistant director of the office of undergraduate admissions
Website: www.augsburg.edu

Admissions Stats

Percentage of applicants admitted: 78.9%
Average GPA range: 3.26 (29 percent have 3.0 or below)
SAT range: 490-610 verbal, 490-610 math
ACT range: 20-25 composite, 19-25 English, 18-25 math

Size

Number of undergraduates: 2,916

Costs

Tuition and fees: $21,960
Books and supplies: $1,000
On campus room and board and other expenses: $6,340
Off campus room and board and other expenses: Varies
Majors offered: More than 50 majors and six graduate programs

---

Academics

Favorite majors: business, management, marketing, education, music, social work, sciences

---

Student Life

The campus: This small, private liberal arts college, affiliated with the Lutheran church, is located only a few blocks from the Mississippi River in a vibrant neighborhood near the University of Minnesota campus. Students take advantage of the Twin Cities' rich resources for internships and service-learning as well as for cultural and recreational activities. The campus has traditional brick buildings with a newer library and a coffee shop serving Starbucks coffee in the student center. A chapel is home to the optional daily 20-minute chapel service and Sunday morning worship service. There are four residence halls, and the campus has the oldest city park in Minneapolis.

The students: Students come from 45 states, 36 foreign countries and 24 tribal nations/reservations. Women predominate at 58.2% of the population.

The B Features

Special Academic Advising is similar to a Study Skills 101 class and introduces students to the liberal arts, including organization, research, study tips and time management. Each student has an academic advisor. The school also offers tutoring labs in math, writing and public speaking. Augsburg also has a special free program called CLASS (Center for Learning and Adaptive Student Services) for students with A.D.D., A.D.H.D. and other learning issues as well as support and specialized services for students with physical disabilities. For admission, the school would like to see a minimum 3.0 GPA, 22 ACT score and 980 SAT score, but it will "make exceptions." Applications are read individually. The school officially states, "Augsburg guarantees opportunities, not diplomas."

Insight

"We are happy to look beyond a simple GPA," says Bethany Bierman, assistant director of the office of undergraduate admissions. "We want to see the potential for leadership in our students. We want to see passion for a cause, whether it be church, community or school." Augsburg likes to see letters of recommendation from teachers. According to Bierman, taking challenging classes, rather than "fluff," makes a huge impact on admission officers. "We are not bound by numbers and do not only recruit valedictorians," she says, "because we are far more concerned about where students go than where they were when they arrived." Bierman adds that the college's vision document says, "Augsburg is braver than many institutions in its acceptance of students with a broad range of abilities and interests. Central to Augsburg's mission is to help students realize their gifts and to develop them to the best of their abilities, whatever their current level of achievement." Augsburg claims that, instead of being an isolated, homogeneous community, an "ivory tower," it is a place that prepares students for successfully living "in the real world."

Augusta State University

Augusta, GA

Address: 2500 Walton Way, Augusta, GA 30904
Phone: 706-737-1632
Admissions email: admissions@aug.edu
Website: www.aug.edu

Admissions Stats

Percentage of applicants admitted: 66.2%
SAT range: 430-540 verbal, 430-540 math
ACT range: 16-20 composite, 15-20 English, 16-21 math

Size

Number of undergraduates: 5,257

Costs

Tuition and fees: $2,702 in state, $9,670 out of state
Books and supplies: $900
On campus room and board and other expenses: $7,300
Off campus room and board and other expenses: $10,446

Academics

Favorite majors: business, management, marketing and related support services, education, social sciences, psychology and communication, journalism and related programs

---

The B Features

Struggling students are encouraged to contact the instructor or department offering the course for names of tutors. Some of the departments offer Help Labs. The Department of Learning Support helps students learn to write, do math, read critically, study effectively (i.e. the fundamentals of English, mathematics, reading and study skills) and to make the best possible use of all campus resources that can help them improve and cope with college-level course work.

Bellarmine University

Louisville, KY

Address: 2001 Newburg Road, Louisville, KY 40205-0671
Phone: 502-452-8131
Admissions email: admissions@bellarmine.edu
Website: www.bellarmine.edu

Admissions Stats

Percentage of applicants admitted: 78.5%
SAT range: 500-610 verbal, 490-610 math
ACT range: 21-26 composite, 21-27 English, 20-26 math

Size

Number of undergraduates: 2,561

Costs

Tuition and fees: $19,950
Books and supplies: $620
On campus room and board and other expenses: $7,820
Off campus room and board and other expenses: $8,358

Academics

Favorite majors: psychology, business, management, marketing and related support services, biological and biomedical sciences, communication, journalism and related programs, health professions and related clinical services

---

The B Features

The Academic Resource Center is the place for help with your classes and college career. There are tutors available for the 100- and 200-level classes, both in individual and group study sessions. The staff at ARC will help analyze your essays to improve grammar, style and formatting.

Bellarmine also offers a one-hour credit course called Freshman Focus. It helps freshmen make the transition to college. This program includes reading, writing, discussion and out-of-class activities. The focus of the course is increasing a student's self-awareness and sense of purpose when it comes to his/her education and making important decisions about academic and social lives. Students are graded (A to F) in this class.

Bowie State University

Bowie, MD

Address: 14000 Jericho Park Road, Bowie, MD 20715
Phone: 301-860-3415
Website: www.bowiestate.edu

Admissions Stats

Percentage of applicants admitted: 44.3%
SAT range: 400-490 verbal, 400-440 math
ACT range: 16-19 composite

Size

Number of undergraduates: 3,988

Costs

Tuition and fees: $5,218 in state, $13,583 out of state
Books and supplies: $2,596
On campus room and board and other expenses: $8,071
Off campus room and board and other expenses: $10,796

Academics

Favorite majors: business, management, marketing and related support services, social sciences, psychology, computer and information sciences and support services and communications technologies/technicians and support services

---
The B Features

The Writing Center helps students in English class assignments. Bowie has a Student Success and Retention Center, whose motto is "Where Your Successful Tomorrow Begins Today." It hopes to help students through programs and activities that "foster student academic, social and personal development." It is focused on helping freshmen transition into college life through a strong first year with placement testing, mentoring and tutorial services.

In addition to these services, Bowie State sponsors the Freshman Seminar course. It is designed to help each student pursue academic excellence and includes lessons about the college's history and its contribution to Maryland. Students learn to critically analyze specific readings that introduce them to concepts in liberal arts and broaden their understanding of global awareness, critical thinking and oral and written communication skills. According to the college, "The goal is for students to become academically, personally and socially successful within and beyond the intellectual community."

Mentoring is popular at Bowie State. Mentors are matched with students to help foster a strong relationship that "promotes academic success, retention and the successful graduation of students." Peer mentors are paired with six freshmen based on academic majors.

KEAP, or Knowledge Enriched through Academic Performance, helps students with issues like poor grades and poor attendance. Students with a GPA of 2.0 or lower are required to take part in KEAP.

Bryant University

Smithfield, RI

Address: 1150 Douglas Pike, Smithfield, RI 02917
Phone: 401-232-6100
Admissions email: admission@bryant.edu
Website: www.bryant.edu

Admissions Stats

Percentage of applicants admitted: 63%
SAT range: 490-570 verbal, 520-610 math
ACT range: 22-25 composite

Size

Number of undergraduates: 2,976

Costs

Tuition and fees: $23,580
Books and supplies: $900
On campus room and board and other expenses: $10,174
Off campus room and board and other expenses: $8,700

Academics

Favorite majors: business, management, marketing and related support services, social sciences, computer and information sciences and support services, communication, journalism and related programs, and English language and literature/letters

---

The B Features

Bryant College offers the Academic Center for Excellence (ACE). Each year, more than 1,600 students use its services to help with class performance. ACE's philosophy is that college students are not born with good study skills and habits. Like anything else in life, they require practice on a regular basis. Even students who have great study skills in high school may find that they need extra help in college because it requires different kinds of skills. According to the college, ACE's primary goal is to "help students become self-reliant, independent, confident learners so that they may successfully meet the demands of their chosen academic curricula." They do this through both a tutoring program and study skills instruction in group sessions provided by a combination of staff, peer tutors and faculty.

Along with ACE, Bryant offers a Writing Center. Here you can learn and polish skills of written communication through one-on-one consultations with staff and tutors, in addition to access to workshops and printed materials.

University of California-Riverside

Riverside, CA

Address: 900 University Avenue, Riverside, CA 92521
Phone: 951-827-3411
Admissions email: discover@pop.ucr.edu
Website: www.ucr.edu

Admissions Stats

SAT range: 450-570 verbal, 490-620 math
ACT range: 18-24 composite, 17-23 English, 18-25 math

Size

Number of undergraduates: 15,282

Costs

Tuition and fees: $6,684 in state, $23,640 out of state
Books and supplies: $1,600
On campus room and board and other expenses: $12,700
Off campus room and board and other expenses: $10,600

Academics

Favorite majors: business, management, marketing and related support services, social sciences, psychology, biological and biomedical sciences, liberal arts and sciences, general studies and humanities

The B Features

Through the Learning Center educators, counselors and advanced students help with academic performance. Any student who is not satisfied with the grade he/she is getting in any class is welcome, including freshmen and students on academic probation. Virtually all services are free.

The center's ACE Program is designed specifically for students who have been placed on academic probation. Students enter into an official agreement with a counselor and are expected to commit to the program. Activities include study groups, study skills sessions and tutoring. There is an emphasis on goal-setting and motivation as well.

The Learning Center offers ASAP, or Assisting Students Academically and Personally. This is a peer counseling program that helps first-year students with academic, educational, personal and social needs. Other assistance programs include a basic skills unit, computer lab, study group program and tutorial assistance and support.

Chowan College

. . . .

Murfreesboro, NC

Address: 200 Jones Drive, Murfreesboro, NC 27855
Phone: 252-398-1236
Admissions email: admissions@chowan.edu
Website: www.chowan.edu

Admissions Stats

Percentage of applicants admitted: 26.5%
SAT range: 370-470 verbal, 380-480 math
ACT range: 14-18 composite

Size

Number of undergraduates: Almost 800

Costs

Tuition and fees: $14,100
Books and supplies: $775
On campus room and board and other expenses: $6,200
Off campus room and board and other expenses: $6,100

Academics

Favorite majors: parks, recreation and leisure and fitness studies, business, management, marketing and related support services, security and protective services, education and communications technologies/technicians and support services

---
The B Features

Chowan offers its entire student body a tutoring program located in the campus library. Students just request a tutor in any area of study by filling out an online tutor request form. Student tutors work one on one with students for free. The service is available four nights a week. Chowan also has Camp 121, a tutoring center that gives students a quiet space for individual studying between the hours of 9 and 5. Individual and group study sessions are frequently held at Camp 121 as well.

University of Cincinnati

Cincinnati, OH

Address: 2624 Clifton Avenue, Cincinnati, OH 45221
Phone: 513-556-1100
Admissions email: admissions@uc.edu
Website: www.uc.edu

Admissions Stats

SAT range: 460-600 verbal, 460-610 math
ACT range: 18-26 composite, 17-25 English, 17-26 math

Size

Number of undergraduates: 19,159

Costs

Tuition and fees: $8,379 in state, $21,351 out of state
Books and supplies: $830
On campus room and board and other expenses: $12,550
Off campus room and board and other expenses: $12,550

Academics

Favorite majors: business, management, marketing and related support services, engineering, visual and performing arts, English language and literature/letters and health professions and related clinical services

The B Features

At UC, helping new students with lower GPAs get up to speed is usually achieved through the Center for Access and Transition. CAT is geared to help students have the knowledge, skills and resources to earn their degree. They help accomplish this through one-on-one advising and individually tailored academic plans. (For an example of this kind of plan, go to the website.) This includes free tutoring and academic skill-enhancing workshops designed to increase GPAs, improve study skills and time management strategies and increase classroom attendance.

Each student working with CAT has an advisor to create the personalized learning agreement. It will show the student how to meet each requirement for his/her major and may include required homework, workshop attendance or use of various campus resources. The plan clearly outlines the student's responsibilities, which commonly include meeting with his/her academic advisor and regular progress reports from instructors.

Free tutoring is available to all UC students and the campus has a Writing Lab and a Math Resource Center for students as well.

College for Lifelong Learning /Granite State College

Concord, NH

Address: 125 North State Street, Concord, NH 03301
Phone: 603-228-3000 X320
Website: www.cll.edu

Admissions Stats

Percentage of applicants admitted: 93.2%
SAT range: Open admissions
ACT range: Open admissions

Size

Number of undergraduates: 1,732

Costs

Tuition and fees: $4,563 in state, $5,043 out of state
Books and supplies: $600
On campus room and board: No on-campus housing
Off campus room and board and other expenses: $9,399

Academics

Favorite majors: liberal arts and sciences, general studies and humanities, business, management, marketing and related support services, multi/interdisciplinary studies, security and protective services and computer and information sciences and support services

The B Features

At this college, recently renamed Granite State, you can design your own bachelor's degree program. Orientation sessions are offered year round, and academic advisors focus on helping prepare for tests, study and take notes. Academic Resource Coordinators provide additional academic services.

Dean College

· ·

Franklin, MA

Address: 99 Main Street, Franklin, MA 02038-1994
Phone: 1-877-TRY-DEAN (877-879-3326)
Admissions email: admission@dean.edu
Admissions contact: Jay Leiendecker, vice president of enrollment services
Website: www.dean.edu

Admissions Stats

Percentage of applicants admitted: 75.1%
Average GPA range: 2.3-2.75
Average SAT range: 390-490 verbal, 380-490 math
Average ACT range: 15-19 composite

Size

Number of undergraduates: 1,339

Costs

Tuition and fees: $22,650
Books and supplies: $600
On campus room and board and other expenses: $9,764
Off campus room and board and other expenses: $9,764

Academics

Majors offered: All are two-year associate programs except for a bachelor's degree in dance. Ten programs are offered, and 98 percent of the 2004 graduates transferred to a four-year college.

Favorite majors: business, performing arts

Student Life

The campus: Dean College was founded 140 years ago as a boarding school. Today, the campus still features 24 old New England buildings with wrought iron fences from the 1800s alongside modern architecture. Covering 100 acres, it is 40 miles from Boston.

The students: More than 90% live in on-campus housing. The student body is 57.1% men and 42.9% women and comes from 26 states and 20 countries.

The B Features

High school transcript, SAT or ACT scores, a guidance counselor recommendation and an essay are required for admission.

Insight

Dean College is "the way there" for many students who will be able to get their bachelor's degrees, according to Jay Leiendecker, vice president of enrollment services. "We improve a student's skills so that they can raise their GPA," he explains. "We encourage counselors, teachers and coaches to learn about students' personalities and motivation and write to their assessment of the student's potential."

Depaul University

. . . .

Chicago, IL

Address: 55 East Jackson, Chicago, IL 60604
Phone: 312-362-8300
Admissions email: admitpu@depaul.edu
Website: www.depaul.edu

Admissions Stats

Percentage of applicants admitted: 68.8%
SAT range: 520-612 verbal, 500-610 math
ACT range: 21-26 composite, 21-27 English, 20-26 math

Size

Number of undergraduates: 14,585

Costs

Tuition and fees: $19,050
Books and supplies: $1,000
On campus room and board and other expenses: $7,895
Off campus room and board and other expenses: $9,585

Academics

Favorite majors: business, management, marketing and related support services, social sciences, education, liberal arts and sciences, general studies and humanities, computer and information sciences and support sciences

The B Features

Student Support Services is open to students who demonstrate a need for academic support and one of the following three requirements: a low income as defined by the U.S. Department of Education, from a family from which neither parent has a bachelor's degree or have a documented physical or learning disability.

SSS provides advising, academic assistance and mentoring to undergrads meeting the above requirements. An advisor is assigned who will help develop an educational plan, select courses and find resources to help with financing your education. SSS also offers individual tutoring and group study opportunities in a variety of subjects. Workshops are offered each quarter to help with learning and topics such as memory, active learning, note taking and test preparation.

Drew University

Address: 36 Madison Avenue, Madison, NJ 07940
Phone: 973-408-3739
Admissions email: cadm@drew.edu
Website: www.drew.edu

Admissions Stats

Percentage of applicants admitted: 69.9%
SAT range: 560-670 verbal, 550-650 math
ACT range: 22-29 composite, 22-31 English, 23-28 math

Size

Number of undergraduates: 1,606

Costs

Tuition and fees: $29,546
Books and supplies: $1,090
On campus room and board and other expenses: $10,456
Off campus room and board and other expenses: $12,072

Academics

Favorite majors: social sciences, psychology, English language and literature/letters, visual and performing arts, multi/interdisciplinary studies

---

The B Features

Peer tutors are available for all courses taught in any given semester. The campus also features a Writing Center where students can learn more about the writing process, as well as bring reports, papers and other written material to get impartial and helpful responses. At the center, they can find out more about organizing papers, the process of revisions, grammar techniques, writing speeches and resumes and looking at proper word choice.

Drexel University

Philadelphia, PA

Address: 3141 Chestnut Street, Philadelphia, PA 19104
Phone: 215-895-2400
Admissions email: enroll@drexel.edu
Website: www.drexel.edu

Admissions Stats

Percentage of applicants admitted: 71%
SAT range: 540-640 verbal, 560-670 math
ACT range: Not available

Size

Number of undergraduates: 11,613

Costs

Tuition and fees: $23,105
Books and supplies: $1,500
On campus room and board and other expenses: $13,050
Off campus room and board and other expenses: $13,525

Academics

Favorite majors: business, management, marketing and related support services, engineering, computer and informational sciences and support services, health professions and related clinical sciences, visual and performing arts

---

The B Features

Free tutoring is available to all students of the College of Nursing and Health Professions, the School of Public Health and non-medical students of the College of Medicine. Some tutoring is individualized, while others are in a group situation.

The Student Counseling Center helps students with personal issues, including making the adjustment to university life. At different times throughout the year, workshops on study skills, stress management, assertiveness training and sexual health are offered. The center provides academic skills testing, and counselors can help establish an individualized time management system, improve study skills and test taking abilities and reduce test anxiety.

Duquesne University

Pittsburgh, PA

Address: Administration Building, Building 600, Forbes Ave., Pittsburgh, PA 15282
Phone: 412-396-6222
Admissions email: admissions@duq.edu
Website: www.duq.edu

Admissions Stats

Percentage of applicants admitted: 85.1%
SAT range: 510-660 verbal, 510-610 math
ACT range: 21-26 composite, 20-26 English, 20-26 math

Size

Number of undergraduates: 5,724

Costs

Tuition and fees: $20,360
Books and supplies: $600
On campus room and board and other expenses: $8,970
Off campus room and board and other expenses: $8,970

Academics

Favorite majors: psychology, business, management, marketing and related support services, communication, journalism and related programs, education and health professions and related clinical sciences

The B Features

At the Michael P. Weber Learning Skills Center, students will find three programs that are designed to help them achieve academic success: Individualized Study Skills Assistance, tutoring and College Success Credit Courses.

Individualized Study Skills Assistance teaches students about reading, note taking, organizing information, listening, test taking and more. It helps you to understand how to learn more effectively and efficiently. Tutoring is done on a one-to-one or small-group basis and is free for all students. Study skills classes can also be taken for college course credit.

Eckerd College

. . . .

St. Petersburg, FL

Address: 4200 54th Avenue South, St. Petersburg, FL 33711-4700
Phone: 727-864-8331
Admissions email: admissions@eckerd.edu
Website: www.eckerd.edu

Admissions Stats

Percentage of applicants admitted: 74.3%
SAT range: 520-630 verbal, 490-600 math
ACT range: 22-27 composite, 21-28 English, 20-26 math

Size

Number of undergraduates: 444

Costs

Tuition and fees: $24,116
Books and supplies: $1,000
On campus room and board and other expenses: $8,976
Off campus room and board and other expenses: $8,976

Academics

Favorite majors: psychology, business, management, marketing and related support services, biological and biomedical sciences, social sciences, natural resources and conservation

The B Features

Eckerd does a number of things differently than other colleges, including support for struggling students. Faculty advisors are much more like mentors and provide continuing support and counsel through the student's years. Freshmen choose a mentor from a list of professionals who lead what is called Autumn Term at Eckerd. First-year students report to the school three weeks before returning students and take part in a course (for credit) that provides a thorough introduction to the campus and its resources as well as academic requirements and policies. Following the freshman year, students can choose a new mentor who specializes in their area of academic interest.

Graduates receive more than the official academic transcript. They also get a co-curricular transcript that includes all of the out-of-class activities the student has been involved in including volunteer work, sports, leadership positions and club involvement. This transcript can be used to supplement applications for jobs, graduate work or other postgraduate plans.

Evergreen State College

Olympia, WA

Address: 2700 Evergreen Parkway Northwest, Olympia, WA 98505
Phone: 360-867-6170
Admissions email: admissions@evergreen.edu
Website: www.evergreen.edu

Admissions Stats

SAT range: 530-650 verbal, 480-600 math
ACT range: 19-27 composite

Size

Number of undergraduates: 4,103

Costs

Tuition and fees: $3,900 in state, $14,514 out of state
Books and supplies: $780
On campus room and board and other expenses: $9,499
Off campus room and board and other expenses: $9,499

Academics

Favorite majors: liberal arts and sciences, general studies and humanities

---

The B Features

Evergreen has a different style of teaching that will appeal to students that do not excel with the typical lecture/listen methods. It designs classes so that there is a balance between seminars, hands-on learning and off-campus exploration. Weeklong field trips are not uncommon here. The college also offers a program called Individual Learning Contracts. This allows students to do advanced academic study in an area they already have a background in, working independently and meeting weekly with a sponsor. Evergreen also has an extensive study abroad program for students.

Fairmont State College

* *

Fairmont, WV

Address: 1201 Locust Avenue, Fairmont, WV 26554
Phone: 304-367-4173
Admissions email: admit@fairmontstate.edu
Website: www.fscwv.edu

Admissions Stats

Percentage of applicants admitted: 77.2%
SAT range: 420-510 verbal, 400-530 math
ACT range: 14-25 composite, 18-26 English, 17-25 math

Size

Number of undergraduates: 4,058

Costs

Tuition and fees: $3,640 in state, $7,874 out of state
Books and supplies: $1,200
On campus room and board and other expenses: $8,554 including transportation and personal expenses
Off campus room and board and other expenses: $10,154 including transportation and personal expenses

---

Academics

Favorite majors: education, business, management, marketing and related support services, security and protective services, liberal arts and sciences, humanities and general studies, engineering technology and technicians

---

The B Features

The student to faculty ratio is about 17:1, and average class size is 22 students. Fairmont is two schools in one. Here you can earn an associate degree through Fairmont State Community and Technical College, then get a bachelor's degree at the university. Tutoring is free for all students through the Tutorial Services Program, although the majority of students are limited to 10 hours per semester. (Students with documented learning disabilities may get additional sessions.) Virtually all subject areas are covered. Fairmont also offers a new program called Supplemental Instruction, designed to help students with courses that have historically proven to be the most difficult. The course is free and is taught by faculty-recommended students.

Fisk University

Nashville, TN

Address: 1000 17th Avenue North, Nashville, TN 37208-4501
Phone: 615-329-8665
Admissions email: admissions@fisk.edu
Website: www.fisk.edu

Admissions Stats

Percentage of applicants admitted: 65.6%
SAT range: 410-540 verbal, 400-500 math
ACT range: 17-21 composite, 16-21 English, 16-20 math

Size

Number of undergraduates: 858

Costs

Tuition and fees: $12,410
Books and supplies: $1,000
On campus room and board and other expenses: $9,750
Off campus room and board and other expenses: $9,730

Academics

Favorite majors: psychology, business, management, marketing and related support services, visual and performing arts, biological and biomedical sciences, social sciences

---
The B Features

The Core Curriculum is really the heart of Fisk's education program. It centers around eight multicultural and interdisciplinary courses and is designed to help students grasp oral and written communication skills, logical and critical thinking, knowledge of the arts, history and literature and the processes and methods of science.

Florida Agricultural and Mechanical University

Tallahassee, FL

Address: Office of Admissions, Foote Hilyer Administration Center, Suite G9 Tallahassee, FL 32307
Phone: 850-599-3796
Admissions email: amd@famu.edu
Website: www.famu.edu

Admissions Stats

Percentage of applicants admitted: 70.7%
SAT range: 440-550 verbal, 440-550 math
ACT range: 19-22 composite, 17-21 English, 20-22 math

Size

Number of undergraduates: 11,164

Costs

Tuition and fees: $2,852 in state, $14,949 out of state
Books and supplies: $1,400
On campus room and board and other expenses: $9,914
Off campus room and board and other expenses: $13,472

Academics

Favorite majors: business, management, marketing and related support services, health professions and related clinical sciences, education, social sciences, security and protective services

The B Features

While academics are very important, Florida A&M also seeks students with diverse backgrounds and considers the other skills and talents students can add to the university. Applicants may demonstrate their strengths through the admission essay.

Full Sail Real World Education

Winter Park, FL

Address: 3300 University Boulevard, Winter Park, FL 32792
Phone: 407-679-6333
Website: www.fullsail.com

Admissions Stats

SAT range: Not required
ACT range: Not required

Size

Number of undergraduates: 4,800

Costs

Tuition and fees: $37,995
Books and supplies: $150
On campus room and board: No on-campus housing
Off campus room and board and other expenses: $12,618

Academics

Favorite majors: computer and information sciences and support services

The B Features

This college is designed for those who are passionate about film, computer animation and design. It has open admissions, meaning all that is required is a high school diploma or GED for admittance. Full Sail specializes in job placement after graduation. There is no on-campus housing, but a department helps place students in available housing throughout the area. Programs start year round. Students attend classes five or six days a week for a total of 35 to 40 hours per week. With this schedule, you finish school much faster than the traditional four-year program. It is one of the only (if not the only) colleges that feature a Guitar Hall of Fame in its buildings.

Goucher College

. . . .

Baltimore, MD

Address: 1021 Dulaney Valley Road, Baltimore, MD 21204-2794
Phone: 410-337-6100
Admissions email: admissions@goucher.edu
Website: www.goucher.edu

Admissions Stats

Percentage of applicants admitted: 67.8%
SAT range: 550-660 verbal, 530-630 math
ACT range: 23-27 composite, 23-29 English, 21-24 math

Size

Number of undergraduates: 1,310

Costs

Tuition and fees: $25,750
Books and supplies: $800
On campus room and board and other expenses: $10,275
Off campus room and board and other expenses: $5,070

Academics

Favorite majors: psychology, social sciences, visual and performing arts, English language and literature/letters, communication, journalism and related programs

---

The B Features

Goucher's Academic Center for Excellence is for all students and is based on the premise that each student has the ability to learn and successfully complete all college course work. Individual help in study skills is provided by mentors, successful students who have been trained in peer counseling. They meet with students one or two times a week. Others work with students on issues like time management, procrastination prevention, organizational skills, memory and concentration, note and test taking strategies and test preparation. Study Skills Workshops are offered repeatedly on these same subjects.

In addition to these services, Goucher offers supplemental instruction in the sciences and humanities. Study groups meet regularly with an instructor and work together as a team to better understand the material. A drop-in Math Lab is offered on campus Sunday through Thursday, and a Writing Center, although not part of ACE, is available to help students at all stages of the writing process.

Grand Canyon University

Phoenix, AZ

Address: 3300 West Camelback Road, Phoenix, AZ 85107
Phone: 602-589-2855
Website: www.gcu.edu

Admissions Stats

Percentage of applicants admitted: 65.9%
SAT range: Open admissions
ACT range: Open admissions

Size

Number of undergraduates: 1,493

Costs

Tuition and fees: $14,500
Books and supplies: $888
On campus room and board and other expenses: $10,092
Off campus room and board and other expenses: $10,324

Academics

Favorite majors: health professions and related clinical services, business, management, marketing and related support services, education, biological and biomedical services, visual and performing arts

The B Features

While the college features open admissions, it has some minimal standards. A minimum GPA of 2.25, a combined SAT score of 920 or above or a composite ACT score of 19 or above are required. The school does have a strongly Christian focus and bills itself as the "University with a Heart" because of its strong commitment to the student-teacher relationship.

Guilford College

. . . .

Greensboro, NC

Address: 5800 West Friendly Avenue, Greensboro, NC 27410
Phone: 336-316-2100
Admissions contact: Tania Johnson, associate director of admissions
Website: www.guilford.edu

Admissions Stats

Percentage of applicants admitted: 63%
Average GPA range: 3.4
SAT range: 520-660 verbal, 510-660 math
ACT range: 21-27 composite

Size

Number of undergraduates: 2,692 (1,289 traditional age 17-22, 81% live on campus; Center for Continuing Education 1,303; Early College 100)

Costs

Tuition and fees: $21,710
Books and supplies: $800
On campus room and board and other expenses: $6,530
Off campus room and board and other expenses: Varies
Degrees offered: bachelor's degrees

Academics

Favorite majors: business, management, marketing and related support services, security and protective services, computer and information sciences and support services, social sciences, psychology

---
Student Life

The campus: This campus is in Greensboro, population 250,000. It has recently added a new community center and residence halls. Guilford was founded by the Religious Society of Friends (Quakers).
The students: 53% women, 48% men. 10% African American, 2% Hispanic, 1% American Indian/Alaskan Native, 2% Asian/Pacific Islander

---
The B Features

At Guilford, the SAT is optional and writing samples and an interview are required when a student does not submit standardized test scores. It is home to a high school preparation school with 100 students. In a required first-year class, students are taken on campus tours, shown various re-sources and helped to transition to college life.

Insight

"Going to college at Guilford is a transformative experience," says Tania Johnson, associate director of admissions. "A quarter of our students go directly to graduate school and half of those that don't do it right after graduation do so within five years."

Although the SAT is optional, other requirements take its place. "We ask for three to five writing samples in lieu of the test scores," says Johnson. "They show us how the student thinks. We also require an interview." Johnson says that the admissions department looks for upward trends in academics throughout high school, as well as extra-curricular involvement, whether it be church, community, sports or jobs. Like some other colleges, admissions recalculates each student's GPA, taking out classes like band, music, home economics and journalism.

"Our unique first year course helps many students," says Johnson. "All students have to take it so there is no stigma. In this class, students are taken on tours all over the campus so they know where to find resources. It also includes a writing intensive course and a great deal of helpful information on developing good study skills. It truly is a great bonding experience for students," she adds. "The teacher of this course is also their academic advisor until they officially declare a major. This advisor helps each student to select the best courses to take.

"Guilford is a place where great education, diversity and an amazing opportunity for growth come together," says Johnson. "Because we are a Quaker-founded institution, the college is guided by Quaker principles that have shaped the college's core values."

Hampton University

Hampton, VA

Address: Hampton, VA 23668-0099
Phone: 757-727-5328
Admissions email: admit@hamptonu.edu
Website: www.hamptonu.edu

Admissions Stats

Percentage of applicants admitted: 53.9%
SAT range: 481-629 verbal, 466-598 math
ACT range: 20-27 composite, 21-28 English, 19-26 math

Size

Number of undergraduates: 4,947

Costs

Tuition and fees: $13,506
Books and supplies: $843
On campus room and board and other expenses: $9,182
Off campus room and board and other expenses: $11,664

Academics

Favorite majors: psychology, business, management, marketing and related support services, communication, journalism and related programs, health professions and related clinical services, social sciences

The B Features

This is a primarily African American college (95.5%). Student Support Services is a federally funded program that, like many others, helps to support students as long as they meet one or more of the three criteria: come from a family where neither parent has a college degree, come from a low-income family or have a documented learning or physical disability. It provides educational support service through counseling, tutoring and educational and career seminars. The overall goal is to "develop and implement educational services and activities that will motivate and assist students toward the achievement of their academic, career, social and personal goals."

University of Hartford

West Hartford, CT

Address: 200 Bloomfield Avenue, West Hartford, CT 06117
Phone: 860-768-4296
Admissions email: admission@mail.hartford.edu
Website: www.hartford.edu

Admissions Stats

Percentage of applicants admitted: 63.7%
SAT range: 480-580 verbal, 490-580 math
ACT range: 20-25 composite

Size

Number of undergraduates: 5,612

Costs

Tuition and fees: $23,480
Books and supplies: $860
On campus room and board and other expenses: $10,346
Off campus room and board and other expenses: $10,346

Academics

Favorite majors: visual and performing arts, business, management, marketing and related support services, communication, journalism and related programs, health professions and related clinical services, education

The B Features

The Center for Reading and Writing (CRW) provides writing tutors that work one on one with students in all phases of writing, from start to finish. Hartford also has a math and physics tutoring lab, chemistry tutors, computer science tutoring labs and on-campus tutoring service that matches new students with trained and experienced student tutors.

The All University Curriculum covers 11 categories of learning, from arts and culture to responsibility for civic life and values identification. These classes are taught through a variety of methods including simulations, debates, field trips, interviews, surveys, discussions, oral reports and skits or dramatic scenes. Students are required to take at least four of these courses over a four-year period.

Hartwick College

Oneonta, NY

Address: One Hartwick Drive, Oneonta, NY 13820-4020
Phone: 607-431-4150
Admissions email: admissions@hartwick.edu
Website: www.hartwick.edu

Admissions Stats

Percentage of applicants admitted: 88.3%
SAT range: 1050-1220 overall
ACT range: 21-27 composite

Size

Number of undergraduates: 369

Costs

Tuition and fees: $20,015
Books and supplies: $700
On campus room and board and other expenses: $7,980
Off campus room and board and other expenses: $5,700

Academics

Favorite majors: psychology, business, management, marketing and related support services, visual and performing arts, biological and biomedical sciences, social sciences

The B Features

Hartwick's Academic Center for Excellence assigns each incoming student to a professional advisor. Together they discuss academic progress and course selection. Other ACE staff members are available to advise students in related areas such as schedule changes and degree planning.

Tutoring is available in most subject areas simply by filling out a request form. Supplemental instructors also help with courses that are considered especially challenging. They organize group tutoring sessions and work one on one inside the classroom.

If a student's overall GPA falls below 2.0, he/she must sign a probationary agreement. All students on probation need to be involved in one of three programs: Close Scrutiny (a weekly one on one with a professional staff member); College Success (a small group weekly meeting to discuss issues of concern and develop strategies for academic success); or regular meetings with professional staff (to ensure students are staying on track).

University of Hawaii at Manoa

Honolulu, HI

Address: 2500 Campus Road, Hawaii Hall, Honolulu, HI 96822
Phone: 808-956-8975
Admissions email: ar-info@hawaii.edu
Website: www.manoa.hawaii.edu

Admissions Stats

Percentage of applicants admitted: 66.8%
SAT range: 480-570 verbal, 510-620 math
ACT range: 20-24 composite, 19-24 English, 20-25 math

Size

Number of undergraduates: 13,753

Costs

Tuition and fees: $3,580 in state, $10,060 out of state
Books and supplies: $1,017
On campus room and board and other expenses: $7,452
Off campus room and board and other expenses: $8,883

Academics

Favorite majors: English language, literature/letters, psychology, business, management, marketing and related support services, social sciences, education

The B Features

The Learning Center has a variety of services including testing, tutoring, study skills information and computer services. Practical skills are taught in areas like speed reading, test taking and time management. Tutoring in math, English, foreign language and other subjects is available by appointment or walk-in. The university also has two computer labs for extra assistance.

High Point University

. . . .

High Point, NC

Address: 833 Montlieu Avenue, High Point, NC 27262
Phone: 336-841-9216
Admissions email: admiss@highpoint.edu
Website: www.highpoint.edu

Admissions Stats

Percentage of applicants admitted: 76.6%
SAT range: 450-560 verbal, 450-560 math
ACT range: Not available

Size

Number of undergraduates: 2,684

Costs

Tuition and fees: $15,700
Books and supplies: $1,000
On campus room and board and other expenses: $9,180
Off campus room and board and other expenses: $9,800

Academics

Favorite majors: business, management, marketing and related support services, computer and information sciences and support services, psychology, education, parks, recreation, leisure and fitness studies

The B Features

The Academic Services Center "strives to foster the academic growth and development" of its students. Tutoring is available at no charge year round. Walk-in tutoring promotes group tutoring; individual tutoring can be scheduled with a simple request form. In additional, supplemental instruction puts a tutor in classrooms to listen and take notes and then help students with those classes. For communication classes, Writing Fellows review students' essays and help them improve.

Hiram College

Hiram, OH

Address: Hinsdale Hall, Third floor, Hiram, OH 44234
Phone: 330-569-5169
Admissions email: admission@hiram.edu
Website: www.hiram.edu

Admissions Stats

Percentage of applicants admitted: 67.9%
SAT range: 510-640 verbal, 490-600 math
ACT range: 20-26 composite, 20-26 English, 19-26 math

Size

Number of undergraduates: 900 residential, 300 enrolled in Weekend College

Costs

Tuition and fees: $22,595
Books and supplies: $600
On campus room and board and other expenses: $7,741
Off campus room and board and other expenses: $11,522

Academics

Favorite majors: psychology, business, management, marketing and related support services, biological and biomedical sciences, social sciences, education

The B Features

Hiram offers hands-on experiences in academics as well as off-campus study programs. Student Academic Services provides a variety of assistance programs including online time management tips and free peer tutoring with fellow students who excel in the class you are struggling with.

The Writing Center offers information, services and programs to help students write more efficiently and effectively as well as to foster a love and respect for language. Trained writing assistants are available by appointment. Along with these services, the college provides test-taking tips.

Hollins University

Roanoke, VA

Address: 7916 Williamson Road Northwest, Roanoke, VA 24020
Phone: 540-362-6401
Admissions email: huadm@hollins.edu
Website: www.hollins.edu

Admissions Stats

Percentage of applicants admitted: 81.9%
SAT range: 550-670 verbal, 500-610 math
ACT range: 22-28 composite

Size

Number of undergraduates: 812

Costs

Tuition and fees: $21,675
Books and supplies: $800
On campus room and board and other expenses: $9,250
Off campus room and board and other expenses: $7,725

Academics

Favorite majors: English language, literature/letters, psychology, social sciences, communication, journalism and related programs, visual and performing arts

The B Features

While this is listed as an all women college, men do account for 4% of the student body. The Center for Learning Excellence is made up of a Writing Center and a Quantitative Reasoning Center.

The Writing Center is there to advise and guide students to understanding the writing process. Students learn about developing thesis statements, finding source materials and doing revisions.

The Quantitative Reasoning Center was originally established in 2002. It is focused on assisting students to improve their reasoning skills. Tutors answer questions about Math 100.

Hood College

. . . .

Frederick, MD

Address: 401 Rosemont Avenue, Frederick, MD 21701
Phone: 301-696-3400
Admissions email: admissions@hood.edu
Website: www.hood.edu

Admissions Stats

Percentage of applicants admitted: 57.1%
SAT range: 490-620 verbal, 490-600 math
ACT range: 20-25 composite

Size

Number of undergraduates: 864

Costs

Tuition and fees: $21,275
Books and supplies: $800
On campus room and board and other expenses: $8,620
Off campus room and board and other expenses: $8,300

Academics

Favorite majors: psychology, business, management, marketing and related support services, biological and biomedical sciences, social sciences, education

---
The B Features

Student-to-faculty ratios are an impressive 10:1 for undergrads. Class sizes are also smaller than the average.

Academic Services focuses on helping students who are having trouble in courses as well as those who just want to be more effective learners. Freshmen and sophomores are advised by a special group of faculty. Once a major is declared they are reassigned to an advisor in that subject.
If math gives you trouble, Hood can evaluate your skills through a Basic Skills Inventory. If you need more work before enrolling in a college math course, you can take algebra review classes. In addition, classroom teaching, tutoring, videos, computer software and printed materials are available. Individualized programs are sometimes offered.

University of Houston at University Park

Houston, TX

Address: University Park, East Cullen, Suite 212, Houston, TX 77024
Phone: 713-743-1010
Admissions email: admissions@uh.edu
Website: www.uh.edu

Admissions Stats

Percentage of applicants admitted: 80.6%
SAT range: 450-570 verbal, 490-600 math
ACT range: 19-23 composite, 17-23 English, 18-25 math

Size

Number of undergraduates: 27,048

Costs

Tuition and fees: $4,082 in state, $10,274 out of state
Books and supplies: $1,150
On campus room and board and other expenses: $10,130
Off campus room and board and other expenses: $13,850

Academics

Favorite majors: business, management, marketing and related support services, psychology, social sciences, engineering, communication, journalism and related programs

The B Features

Learning and Assessment Services offers workshops covering topics such as improving memory power, overcoming procrastination, reducing test anxiety, preparing for exams and time management. Tutoring is available for free on both a walk-in and appointment basis. Multimedia Resources can help students who learn best on the computer, and math, science and business majors can find supplemental instruction study groups that meet on a regular basis. The Texas Success Initiative Program provides non-course, non-credit developmental instruction in reading, writing, math and test preparation.

Howard University

Washington, DC

Address: 2400 Sixth Street Northwest, Washington, DC 20059-0001
Phone: 202-806-2763
Admissions email: admissions@howard.edu
Website: www.howard.edu

Admissions Stats

Percentage of applicants admitted: 46.9%
SAT range: 430-690 verbal, 450-680 math
ACT range: 18-29 composite

Size

Number of undergraduates: 7,059

Costs

Tuition and fees: $11,645
Books and supplies: $1,020
On campus room and board and other expenses: $7,670
Off campus room and board and other expenses: $13,463

Academics

Favorite majors: business, management, marketing and related support services, biological and biomedical sciences, health professions and related clinical services, computer and information science and support services, communication and journalism and related programs

---

The B Features

A predominantly African American college (68.7%), Howard assigns undergraduates an academic advisor during their first week of school.

The Center for Academic Reinforcement assists students with academic difficulties, conducts pre-orientation programs for entering freshmen, offers three-credit-hour courses in mathematics, verbal, study skills and reading and recently provided 2,000 tutoring and laboratory assistance sessions.

University of Idaho

Moscow, ID

Address: 875 Perimeter Drive, Moscow, ID 83844
Phone: 208-885-6326
Admissions email: admappl@uidaho.edu
Website: www.uidaho.edu

Admissions Stats

Percentage of applicants admitted: 82.7%
SAT range: 480-610 verbal, 490-610 math
ACT range: 20-26

Size

Number of undergraduates: 9,484

Costs

Tuition and fees: $3,632 in state, $11,652 out of state
Books and supplies: $1,286
On campus room and board and other expenses: $8,382
Off campus room and board and other expenses: $8,382

Academics

Favorite majors: business, management, marketing and related support services, communication, journalism and related programs, education, natural resources and conservation

The B Features

Three academic assistance programs are offered. Tutoring and Learning Services offers one-on-one tutoring as well as a series of workshops called The College Success Series. These workshops cover such areas as Active Note Taking, the Cycle of Active Learning, College Textbook Reading and Time Management. Freshmen are also offered a one-credit study skills course, and there is an online learning center as well. Students in accounting, computer science and chemistry have their own learning labs and study groups and there is a separate Math Lab. The English Writing Center helps with all facets of written communication.

Student Support Services is designed to provide academic support and assistance to students who meet the TRIO eligibility standards (neither parent has a college degree, or they come from a low-income family or they are physically/learning disabled.) The Disability Support Services is geared to assist students that are physically challenged as defined by the American Disabilities Act.

Indiana State University

Terre Haute, IN

Address: 210 North 7th Street, Terre Haute, IN 47809
Phone: 812-237-2121
Website: www.indstate.edu

Admissions Stats

Percentage of applicants admitted: 83.3%
SAT range: 420-520 verbal, 420-530 math
ACT range: 17-22 composite, 16-22 English, 17-23 math

Size

Number of undergraduates: 9,615

Costs

Tuition and fees: $5,640 in state, $12,368 out of state
Books and supplies: $1,020
On campus room and board and other expenses: $8,152
Off campus room and board and other expenses: $9,444

Academics

Favorite majors: business, management, marketing and related support services, education, social sciences, engineering technologies/technicians, visual and performing arts

---

The B Features

The Student Academic Services Center helps in several ways. The Mentoring Program's primary goal, according to the college, is to "assist first-year students so that they may benefit from additional support, encouragement and services." Staff members are updated weekly on each student's progress and adjustment to college life. Students sign a Mentoring Contract at the beginning of the process.

A professional advisement staff is always available for further help or advice. The school offers a tutoring program for all general studies classes on either a drop-in or appointment basis. Additionally, students are invited to take University 101-Learning in the University Community, a two-credit hour elective that helps with the transition to the college. It teaches study strategies, critical thinking and writing skills and introduces students to campus resources and services and discusses the history of the school and the community around it.

Indiana University at Bloomington

Bloomington, IN

Address: Bryan Hall, Bloomington, IN 47405
Phone: 812-855-0661
Admissions email: iuadmit@indiana.edu
Website: www.iu.edu

Admissions Stats

Percentage of applicants admitted: 83%
SAT range: 490-600 verbal, 500-620 math
ACT range: 22-27 composite, 21-28 English, 21-27 math

Size

Number of undergraduates: 30,319

Costs

Tuition and fees: $6,777 in state, $18,590 out of state
Books and supplies: $740
On campus room and board and other expenses: $11,320
Off campus room and board and other expenses: $11,320

Academics

Favorite majors: business, management, marketing and related support services, biological and biomedical sciences, communication, journalism and related programs, education, public administration and social service professions

The B Features

The Student Academic Center is focused on helping with any problems they are having. According to the college, its philosophy is "student support, student respect and student success."

Study Smarter Workshops cover a wide field of topics for students including Learning from your Returned Exam, Improving Reading Speed and Catching Up in a Course When All Hope Seems Gone.

Supplemental Instruction offers small group study sessions guided by fellow students who have already taken the same course and been recommended by the professor. Here, students can review content, ask questions, discuss issues and learn effective reading and study strategies.

The Phoenix Program serves students who have been put on academic probation. It offers several courses to help get them back on track. Those that do are later offered the chance to serve as peer mentors to others.

Individualized Academic Assessment and Assistance is offered to students who are not sure about their strengths and weaknesses or exactly what kind of help they need. This free assessment program is done on a walk-in or appointment basis.

Outreach Services is a program of mini-workshops or presentations that are offered in the residence halls, fraternity houses, classes or organizations on topics such as test taking and time management.

Non-Credit Programs and Services is an hour-long, individual session that can help students identify and target areas causing academic stress.

The Right Start Program is for freshmen who are not familiar with campus/college life (first-generation students, small towns or high schools, etc.). It offers an orientation to the college life and culture of IU through resources in small seminar groups. A full semester, it earns two credit hours and teaches lessons about the campus, college lifestyles and study skills.

Indiana University of Pennsylvania

Indiana, PA

Address: 1011 South Drive, 201 Sutton Hall, Indiana, PA 15705
Phone: 724-357-2230
Admissions email: admissions-inquiry@iup.edu
Website: www.iup.edu

Admissions Stats

Percentage of applicants admitted: 59.6%
SAT range: 480-570 verbal, 470-570 math
ACT range: Not available

Size

Number of undergraduates: 12,119

Costs

Tuition and fees: $6,085 in state, $13,351 out of state
Books and supplies: $800
On campus room and board and other expenses: $7,815
Off campus room and board and other expenses: $7,815

Academics

Favorite majors: business, management, marketing and related support services, social sciences, education, visual and performing arts, communication, journalism and related programs

The B Features

Credit courses help students cope with the demands of college. Through the Learning Enhancement Center, a student can take classes on such topics as Learning Strategies, Vocabulary Expansion, Reading Skills for College Study and Introduction to College Math 1. The center provides tutoring, supplemental instruction, workshops and a campus-wide academic support program to help all levels of students.

The Writing Center offers tutoring by other students on a drop-in basis. The center also sponsors writing workshops with subjects such as Using the Internet for Academic Research and Resume Writing.

If a student's GPA falls below 2.0, he/she is placed on academic probation and must implement an Academic Recovery Plan.

University of Louisiana at Lafayette

Lafayette, LA

Address: 104 University Circle, Lafayette, LA 70503
Phone: 377-482-6467
Admissions email: admissions@louisiana.edu
Website: www.louisiana.edu

Admissions Stats

Percentage of applicants admitted: 85%
SAT range: Not available
ACT range: 18-24 composite, 18-25 English, 17-24 math

Size

Number of undergraduates: 14,585

Costs

Tuition and fees: $3,228 in state, $9,408 out of state
Books and supplies: $1,000
On campus room and board and other expenses: $5,802
Off campus room and board and other expenses: $10,037

Academics

Favorite majors: business, management, marketing and related services, education, engineering, health professions and related clinical services, liberal arts and sciences, general studies and humanities

The B Features

Students may be admitted through the university's Guaranteed Admission requirements, which are:

Completion of the Louisiana Board of Regents' high school core curriculum and a mathematics ACT score of at least 18 (430 Math SAT) or an English ACT score of at least 18 (450 Verbal SAT) and one of the following:

- high school GPA of 2.5 or higher using an unweighted 4.0 scale,

- ACT composite score of at least 23 (SAT 1060) with at least a 2.0 GPA or

- rank in the top 25% of the high school graduating class and at least a 2.0 GPA

Students who don't meet the Guaranteed Admission requirements may apply for Admission by Committee by submitting a completed application.

The Learning Center offers walk-in tutoring, although appointments are sometimes recommended. The Writing Center helps students with all stages of the writing process. Free online tutoring is another service offered through Smart Thinking. With it, students can access live tutorials in writing, math, accounting, statistics and economics. They can also consult writing manuals, sample problems, research tools and study skills manuals.

Study groups are available on campus so that several students can get help on a weekly basis. They are student led, and sessions cover problems and questions from that week's class material.

Study skills and time management skills are found on the college website, including information on reading, note taking, studying, test anxiety, test taking and general study skills.

The college also offers a Career Counseling Center to help you decide on a major. A career counselor is there to guide students to resources and informational material. Along with this, a half-semester, one-credit course on career decision making helps students who want an in-depth career analysis.

Lynn University

Boca Raton, FL

Address: 3601 North Military Trail, Boca Raton, FL 33431
Phone: 561-237-7900
Website: www.lynn.edu

Admissions Stats

Percentage of applicants admitted: 79.5%
SAT range: 400-500 verbal, 390-510 math
ACT range: Not available

Size

Number of undergraduates: 1,928

Costs

Tuition and fees: $23,500
Books and supplies: $950
On campus room and board and other expenses: $10,800
Off campus room and board and other expenses: $10,800

Academics

Favorite majors: business, management, marketing and related support services, psychology, communication, journalism and related programs, visual and performing arts, security and protective services

The B Features

The Institute for Achievement and Learning centers around personalized education. The college states that the institute "embraces, empowers and engages its students to offer opportunities for greater accomplishments in higher education and career realization." Programs include First Year Experience, Tutoring Center, Discovery Writing Center, Metamorphosis Coaching, Probationary Support and Academic Status Support. First Year Experience is required of all freshmen. The two-semester academic program connects new students with peers, campus resources and faculty. In the first class (FYE-1), students focus on the nature of education including units on time management, test taking, communication skills, study techniques, university policies and procedures, resources and services, health and wellness issues and personal issues. FYE-1 also includes a pre-orientation to Academic Adventure, a faculty-led program in which the entire freshman class spends five days in the Caribbean on a ship studying the region's cultures and people. In FYE-2, students explore multicultural and diversity awareness, educational planning, career development, leadership, community service and learning potential—plus reflect upon their Academic Adventure!

The Discovery Writing Center offers one-on-one tutoring for all levels of writing skills. The Hannifan Center for Career Development and Internships provides personalized career counseling, group career workshops, internships and job-placement assistance.

Academic Status Support assists students on academic probation. This free program includes advising and learning strategy suggestions to help students improve their grades. Probationary Support is similar and offers free advising, group tutoring, social activities, counseling sessions and workshops.

Metamorphosis Coaching is geared to students who learn best from hands-on experience rather than traditional classroom methods. It takes students out of the classroom and into such settings as the campus butterfly garden or a local nature center as they learn observation skills logged into journals. According to the college, this program is not just about studying nature, but it also is "a study of life and the nature of our own selves. The 'lessons' learned through this reflective process will provide valuable insights about the way you learn best—and yourself." The program also includes group dinners and guest lecturers as well as private tutoring and field trips. (There is a charge for this program.)

McKendree College

Lebanon, IL

Address: 701 College Road, Lebanon, IL 62254
Phone: 618-537-4481 ext. 6831
Admissions email: inquiry@mckendree.edu
Admissions contact: Mark Campbell, vice president for enrollment management
Website: www.mckendree.edu

Admissions Stats

Percentage of applicants admitted: 70.8%
Average GPA range: 3.6
SAT range: 420-530 verbal, 430-630 math
ACT range: 20-26 composite, 19-26 English, 19-26 math

Size

Number of undergraduates: 1,350 on main campus

Costs

Tuition and fees: $17,500
Books and supplies: $1,000
On campus room and board and other expenses: $7,660
Off campus room and board and other expenses: $7,540
Degrees offered: master's, bachelor's

Academics

Favorite majors: business, management, marketing and related support services, health professions and related clinical services, education, social sciences, computer and information sciences and support services

Student Life

The campus: McKendree has a main campus and three satellite campuses at Scott Air Force Base and two in Kentucky. It is the oldest college in Illinois and was founded in 1828 by "circuit riding Methodists." Twenty five minutes east of the St. Louis Arch, the campus integrates the old and new with buildings that range from 1820 to the new $10 million arts center.

The students: Women are in the majority (55%); about 80% of the student body is white/non-Hispanic.

The B Features

The college features small classes, is eager to accept students who are really trying and is dedicated to not letting any of them "slip through the cracks."

Insight

"McKendree is the only place in southern Illinois where you have an average class size of 15 and all classes are under 50," explains Mark Campbell vice president for enrollment management. "This size helps students to feel less anonymous.

"We do not evaluate students with multiple-choice tests," he adds. "Instead, we want to see how you write. There is a real gray area between students who are easy to admit and those who are easy to deny. The key is in the students' strength in English. How do they read, write and comprehend?" All students who are admitted must submit a writing sample before they are placed in an English class.

"All potential students are invited to write an essay for us," explains Campbell. "We even allow graded papers from school. In the end, we are obligated to not admit students who will not do well. We simply focus on a student's determination to succeed."

University of Maine (Orono)

Orono, ME

Address: 5713 Chadbourne, Orono, ME 04469
Phone: 207-581-1561
Admissions email: um-admit@umaine.edu
Website: www.umaine.edu

Admissions Stats

Percentage of applicants admitted: 75.9%
SAT range: 480-590 verbal, 490-600 verbal
ACT range: 20-27 composite

Size

Number of undergraduates: 8,972

Costs

Tuition and fees: $6,338 in state, $15,658 out of state
Books and supplies: $700
On campus room and board and other expenses: $8,012
Off campus room and board and other expenses: $8,012

Academics

Favorite majors: business, management, marketing and related support services, social sciences, education, health professions and related clinical sciences, engineering

The B Features

The Tutor Program is for small groups who need help in their 100- and 200-level, non-web-based courses. Peer tutors meet with students two or three times a week throughout the semester. This free service is open to any student who has registered for at least six credit hours as well as students who need help in math classes. For those needing help with writing, the Writing Center is there to give advice as well. One student is quoted on the website as saying, "I was not grasping the problems in lecture and I was often confused on which technique to apply. Having students explain ideas and concepts to each other has been very helpful. I have had to be prepared for each session, which keeps me on task."

Marymount Manhattan College

New York, NY

Address: 221 East 71st Street, New York, NY 10021
Phone: 1-800-MARYMOUNT or 212-517-0430
Admissions email: admissions@mmm.edu
Website: www.mmm.edu

Admissions Stats

Percentage of applicants admitted: 79.6%
Average GPA range: 3.2
SAT range: 490-600 verbal, 460-560 math
ACT range: 21-24 composite, 20-26 English, 22-26 math

Size

Number of undergraduates: 2,100

Costs

Tuition and fees: $17,412
Books and supplies: $1,000
On campus room and board and other expenses: $12,920
Off campus room and board and other expenses: $14,066

Academics

Favorite majors: visual and performing arts, communication, journalism and related programs, business, management, marketing and related support services, psychology, social sciences

The B Features

If any of Marymount's students run into problems in a course, the college offers a tutoring center that provides full support with student tutors as well as trained staff on a walk-in basis. The Center for Academic Advancement (formerly known as College Skills) has courses for students who need to reinforce their skills in reading comprehension, vocabulary, grammar and basic writing. According to the college, "It is our mission to provide these services in any reasonable manner in order to secure student futures. Our main objective is to assure each student who passes through our doors that they can and will succeed in college."

George Mason University

Fairfax, VA

Address: 4400 University Drive, Fairfax, VA 22030-4444
Phone: 703-993-2400
Admissions email: admissions@gmu.edu
Website: www.gmu.edu

Admissions Stats

Percentage of applicants admitted: 68.6%
SAT range: 490-600 verbal, 500-600 math
ACT range: Not available

Size

Number of undergraduates: 17,073

Costs

Tuition and fees: $5,448
Books and supplies: $940
On campus room and board and other expenses: $7,435
Off campus room and board and other expenses: $11,913

Academics

Favorite majors: business, management, marketing and related support services, English language and literature/letters, social sciences, psychology, health professions and related clinical services.

The B Features

Learning Services encompasses many different methods to help support students who are struggling academically. Study skills workshops are offered on topics like Improving Concentration, Overcoming Procrastination, Crash Course in Academic Skills and Motivation and Goal Setting. Tutor Referral matches students with peer tutors (which charge varying fees). Services are confidential, and use of these services does not become part of the student's academic record.

The college also offers a Certificate in Academic Skills to help students study more effectively, improve test-taking skills, decrease anxiety about performance and improve grades. Through this process, students go to workshops, listen to audiotapes, watch videotapes, use interactive computer programs and get books from the Self-Help Resource library.

Manhattanville College

. . . .

Purchase, NY

Address: 2900 Purchase Street, Purchase, NY 10577
Phone: 800-328-4553
Admissions email: admissions@mville.edu
Website: www.manhattanville.edu

Admissions Stats

Percentage of applicants admitted: 56.2%
SAT range: 480-610 verbal, 470-600 math
ACT range: 17-24 composite

Size

Number of undergraduates: 1,671

Costs

Tuition and fees: $23,620
Books and supplies: $800
On campus room and board and other expenses: $11,230
Off campus room and board and other expenses: $11,230

Academics

Favorite majors: business, management, marketing and related support services, social sciences, visual and performing arts, psychology, English language and literature/letters

---

The B Features

The Academic Resource Center offers individual tutoring, group supplemental instruction and a variety of workshops. ARC has full-time professional instructors in writing, math and study strategies and part-time tutors in subjects including accounting, foreign languages, math, music theory, statistics for social sciences and economic statistics. Special credit-bearing courses are offered to help students learn science, math and the humanities. According to the college, the philosophy of the ARC is one of "fostering independence in the students who seek help. We are equipped to deal with many types of academic difficulties and to offer personal assistance in a relaxed and supportive atmosphere."

Michigan State University

East Lansing, MI

Address: 250 Administration Building, East Lansing, MI 48824
Phone: 517-355-8332
Admissions email: admissions@msu.edu
Website: www.msu.edu

Admissions Stats

Percentage of applicants admitted: 79.4%
SAT range: 490-620 verbal, 515-650 math
ACT range: 22-27 composite, 21-27 English, 21-27 math

Size

Number of undergraduates: 34,853

Costs

Tuition and fees: $6,999 in state, $17,844 out of state
Books and supplies: $826
On campus room and board and other expenses: $6,922
Off campus room and board and other expenses: $6,922

Academics

Favorite majors: business, management, marketing and related support services, communication, journalism and related programs, social sciences, engineering, biological and biomedical sciences

The B Features

The Learning Resources Center offers help to students looking to improve their grades, develop study strategies and help their overall scholastic performance. It features a professional staff, interactive learning lab and tutoring services in the residence halls. Daytime tutoring is offered in one-hour individual sessions for free, and evening tutoring is available for math groups twice a week. Seminars and workshops are also offered on topics such as test taking and preparing for finals.

Mills College

Oakland, CA

Address: 5000 MacArthur Boulevard, Oakland, CA 94613
Phone: 800-876-4557
Admissions email: admissions@mills.edu
Website: www.mills.edu

Admissions Stats

Percentage of applicants admitted: 82.9%
SAT range: 540-670 verbal, 490-610 math
ACT range: 19-27 composite

Size

Number of undergraduates: 735

Costs

Tuition and fees: $27,085
Books and supplies: $930
On campus room and board and other expenses: $11,029
Off campus room and board and other expenses: $11,079

Academics

Favorite majors: English language, literature/letters, social services, psychology, visual and performing arts, area, ethnic, cultural and gender studies

The B Features

A Writing Center provides help for students who need help to develop their skills. It is staffed by graduate students from the English Department, and one-on-one tutoring is available. In addition, workshops on writing are offered throughout the entire school year. Classes are commonly 20 students or less, and the student-to-faculty ratio is 10:1.

University of Mississippi

University, MS

Address: 145 Martindale, University, MS 38677
Phone: 662-915-7226
Admissions email: admissions@olemiss.edu
Website: www.olemiss.edu

Admissions Stats

Percentage of applicants admitted: 80.9%
SAT range: Not available
ACT range: 20-26 composite, 20-28 English, 18-25 math

Size

Number of undergraduates: 11,224

Costs

Tuition and fees: $4,110 in state, $9,264 out of state
Books and supplies: $900
On campus room and board and other expenses: $8,594
Off campus room and board and other expenses: $8,594

Academics

Favorite majors: business, management, marketing and related support services, education, social sciences, psychology, health professions and related clinical services

The B Features

The Academic Support Center aids struggling students and those who have not yet declared a major. It helps with scheduling classes, exploring possible majors and fulfilling core degree requirements for a bachelor's degree. In addition, the center assists with questions or problems with your schedule, understanding university policies and procedures and providing referrals to other offices if needed.

Mitchell College

New London, CT

Address: 437 Pequot Avenue, New London, CT 06320
Phone: 800-243-2811
Admissions email: hodges_k@mitchell.edu
Admissions contact: Kevin Mayne, vice president for enrollment management and marketing
Website: www.mitchell.edu

Admissions Stats

Percentage of applicants admitted: 61.2%
Average GPA: 2.75
SAT range: 420-470 verbal, 400-450 math
ACT range: 17-19 composite

Size

Number of undergraduates: 780

Costs

Tuition and fees: $19,405
Books and supplies: $1,000
On campus room and board and other expenses: $10,630
Off campus room and board and other expenses: $10,630

Academics

Majors offered: Offering two- and four-year programs, Mitchell has seven bachelor's degrees (business administration, criminal justice, early childhood education, human development and family studies, liberal and professional studies, psychology and sport management) and 12 associate's degree programs (business administration/management, criminal justice, early childhood education, graphic design, human development and family studies, human services, liberal arts (nine divisions), physical education, physical education/health fitness, sport management and undecided/discovery program.)

Student Life

The campus: Located on 65 acres along the Connecticut shoreline, Mitchell has two beaches, athletic fields and wooded trails. Of the seven residence halls, four of them are waterfront Victorian homes. It was founded in 1938 and is two hours from Boston and New York City.

The students: They come from 22 states and 18 countries. The ratio is 49.2% men and 50.8% women with a little over a third of the total population students of color.

The B Features

Admission requirements include high school transcripts, letters of recommendation, personal statement/essay and SAT or ACT scores. An interview is not required but highly recommended. The Career and Academic Program is designed for students who are unsure about their majors. More information is available online.

In fall 2006, Mitchell will also offer an unusual pre-college experience called Thames Academy. This year long program will offer high school graduates academic support through a highly structured and innovative format. Thames Academy hopes to help new students improve their study skills, increase their confidence, strengthen their academics and ease the adjustment to being away from home. During this year, students can earn up to 18 college credits. They are offered content tutoring by a variety of professionals, workshops on core subjects and study skills and a Personalized Learning Plan. Those that are enrolled in this program (the number is limited) are housed and taught separately from the rest of the college population.

Insight

"At Mitchell, we definitely look beyond the numbers," says Kevin Mayne, vice president for enrollment management and marketing. "We always say that we don't judge you by how you do on a Saturday morning with a number 2 pencil in your hand. We take a long time to evaluate each potential student." Mayne explains that admissions does look at the numbers but also the level of the classes and most importantly, "the student's motivation and potential for academic success." Admissions considers what activities the students are involved in, from clubs, sports and organizations to hobbies and community service as well as the overall academic pattern. "Life is a journey," says Mayne, "and we want to help our students to get from point A to point B in their quest for an education. We want to help them find their intent and purpose and then turn on the switch. We love working with average students because they are the ones you will remember most on graduation day. Your heart will be in your throat as they cross the stage, and there won't be a dry eye in the house."

Montana Tech of the University of Montana

Butte, MT

Address: 1300 West Park Street, Butte, MT 59701
Phone: 406-496-4178
Admissions email: admissions@mtech.edu
Website: www.mtech.edu

Admissions Stats

Percentage of applicants admitted: 99.3%
SAT range: 460-600 verbal, 510-620 math
ACT range: 21-27 composite, 17-23 English, 18-26 math

Size

Number of undergraduates: 1,846

Costs

Tuition and fees: $4,531 in state, $13,335 out of state
Books and supplies: $800
On campus room and board and other expenses: $8,328
Off campus room and board and other expenses: $8,328

Academics

Favorite majors: business, management, marketing and related support services, biological and biomedical sciences, English, health professions and related clinical services and computer and information sciences and support services

The B Features

The Montana Tech Learning Center helps students reach their full academic potential through several methods. Approximately 35 to 40% of the full-time students use TLC's resources every semester. Tutors are available in math, science, engineering and environmental courses. Self-tutorial programs are accessible through videotape instruction in math, chemistry, biology, physics, speech, study skills, time management, test anxiety, note taking and stress management. The college also offers a two-credit study/life skills class that focuses on success in school and life. All freshmen are encouraged to take this class.

Morehouse College

Atlanta, GA

Address: 830 Westview Drive Southwest, Atlanta, GA 30314
Phone: 404-215-2632
Admissions email: admissions@morehouse.edu
Website: www.morehouse.edu

Admissions Stats

Percentage of applicants admitted: 67.5%
SAT range: 470-580 verbal, 470-590 math
ACT range: 19-24 composite, 17-24 English, 18-25 math

Size

Number of undergraduates: 643

Costs

Tuition and fees: $15,740
Books and supplies: $850
On campus room and board and other expenses: $12,548
Off campus room and board and other expenses: $12,800

Academics

Favorite majors: psychology, business, management, marketing and related support services, biological and biomedical sciences, social sciences, computer and information science and support services

The B Features

Morehouse is an African American (93%) college for men. The Wellness Resource Center offers personal counseling to help students "resolve personal difficulties and acquire the skills, attitudes and knowledge that will enable them to take full advantage of their experiences at Morehouse College."

University of Nevada-Las Vegas

Las Vegas, NV

Address: 4505 South Maryland Parkway, Las Vegas, NV 89154
Phone: 702-895-3443
Admissions email: undergraduate.recruitment@ccmail.nevada.edu
Website: www.unlv.edu

Admissions Stats

Percentage of applicants admitted: 80.1%
SAT range: 450-560 verbal, 450-580 math
ACT range: 18-24 composite, 17-23 English, 17-24 math

Size

Number of undergraduates: 20,836

Costs

Tuition and fees: $3,270 in state, $11,944 out of state
Books and supplies: $850
On campus room and board and other expenses: $10,658
Off campus room and board and other expenses: $11,530

Academics

Favorite majors: psychology, business, management, marketing and related support services, social science, communication, journalism and related programs, education

The B Features

Student Support Services helps students "overcome personal concerns, academic deficiencies and financial difficulties that could impair their chances of succeeding in college." It focuses on the development of good study habits and decision-making skills through tutoring and workshops on subjects such as study skills, time management, note taking, listening skills, reading and outlining textbooks, test-taking strategies, motivation, concentration and stress reduction. These services are free. An academic enrichment program for high school students called Upward Bound offers academic counseling, career exploration, tutoring, college admission testing workshops, motivation, personal development and concentration in computer literacy, English, foreign language, history, government, math and science. Upward Bound students are often involved in weekend or after-school instruction. During the summer, they can participate in daily classes emphasizing academic skills, study techniques and test preparation.

University of New Mexico

Albuquerque, NM

Address: Office of Recruitment Services, Student Services Center,
Room 180, Albuquerque, NM 87131
Phone: 505-277-2446
Admissions email: apply@unm.edu
Website: www.unm.edu

Admissions Stats

Percentage of applicants admitted: 75.6%
SAT range: 470-600 verbal, 460-590 math
ACT range: 19-24 composite, 18-25 English, 17-24 math

Size

Number of undergraduates: 17,932

Costs

Tuition and fees: $3,738 in state, $12,500 out of state
Books and supplies: $792
On campus room and board and other expenses: $8,534
Off campus room and board and other expenses: $11,010

Academics

Favorite majors: business, management, marketing and related support services, social science, education, liberal arts and sciences, general studies and humanities, health professions and related clinical services

---

The B Features

The Center for Academic Program Support offers free educational assistance through individualized peer tutoring (upper division undergraduates and graduate students) for courses numbered 100-499 as well as library and study strategies (by appointment only). Drop-in tutoring labs are available for biology, chemistry, physics, astronomy, writing, precalculus, statistics, calculus and engineering. In a new program called CAPS Across Campus, tutoring will be offered in the theater, library and student resident center commons room.

University of New Orleans

New Orleans, LA

Address: Lakefront Campus, 2000 Lakeshore Drive, New Orleans, LA 70148
Phone: 504-280-6595
Admissions email: admissions@uno.edu
Website: www.uno.edu

Admissions Stats

Percentage of applicants admitted: 63.4%
SAT range: 450-590 verbal, 450-580 math
ACT range: 18-23

Size

Number of undergraduates: 13,338

Costs

Tuition and fees: $3,184 in state, $10,228 out of state
Books and supplies: $1,000
On campus room and board and other expenses: $7,006
Off campus room and board and other expenses: $10,037

Academics

Favorite majors: business, management, marketing and related support services, communication, journalism and related programs, education, liberal arts and sciences, general studies and humanities, engineering

The B Features

The Learning Resource Center offers free tutoring on both an individual and group basis in writing and math. A computer lab has 24 workstations, and tutors are available in biology, business, chemistry, foreign language, psychology and physics. Much of the tutoring is performed by upperclassmen. Classes on time management, test taking, note taking and communication are offered, as are short workshops on test taking and note taking. A media library supplies videotapes and CD ROMs in math, science and liberal arts.

UNO's Writing Center guides students through their papers, while the Math Tutor Center and Study Hall assists students in math requirements and to "maximize their math potential."

University of North Carolina at Greensboro

Greensboro, NC

Address: 1000 Spring Garden Street, Greensboro, NC 27402
Phone: 336-334-5243
Admissions email: undergrad_admissions@uncg.edu
Website: www.uncg.edu

Admissions Stats

Percentage of applicants admitted: 76.8%
SAT range: 470-570 verbal, 470-570 math
ACT range: 18-23 composite, 17-23 English, 17-23 math

Size

Number of undergraduates: 11,242

Costs

Tuition and fees: $3,435 in state, $14,403 out of state
Books and supplies: $1,463
On campus room and board and other expenses: $7,631
Off campus room and board and other expenses: $9,656

Academics

Favorite majors: business, management, marketing and related support services, social sciences, education, visual and performing arts, health professions and related clinical services

---

The B Features

The Student Success Center has three divisions to help students succeed academically.

The Learning Assistance Center provides tutoring, academic skills assessment and counseling, academic workshops and a resource lab with computers, academic software and handouts. Tutoring is done on an individual basis for at least one hour a week or through small groups of no more than three students 1 1/2 to two hours a week. Walk-in tutoring is available also.

The Resource Lab gives students a peaceful place to study and tutor. Students have access to computers, a text book library, academic skills assessment, computer tutorials in math and foreign languages and handouts on academic skills like time management, note taking, textbook reading and test taking. In addition to this, the LAC works to help students increase their understanding of course content, enhance self-confidence and encourage positive attitudes toward learning.

Special Support Services is for students who are first-generation, from low-income families or who have a documented disability. It offers counseling, tutoring and a learning lab.

Supplemental Instruction is a series of weekly discussion/review sessions for students taking notoriously difficult courses. The class is led by students who have successfully completed the course. According to the college, students who attend these courses attain one-third to one whole grade better than those who do not.

Ohio University

Athens, OH

Address: Undergraduate Admissions, 120 Chubb Hall, Athens, OH 45701-2979
Phone: 740-593-4100
Admissions email: admissions.freshmen@ohiou.edu
Website: www.ohio.edu

Admissions Stats

Percentage of applicants admitted: 86.3%
SAT range: 490-600 verbal, 490-600 math
ACT range: 20-25 composite, 19-25 English, 19-25 math

Size

Number of undergraduates: 17,200

Costs

Tuition and fees: $7,770 in state, $16,734 out of state
Books and supplies: $840
On campus room and board and other expenses: $10,224
Off campus room and board and other expenses: $10,224

Academics

Favorite majors: business, management, marketing and related support services, social sciences, communications, journalism and related programs, education, liberal arts and sciences, general studies and humanities

---

The B Features

The Academic Advancement Center helps prepare students for college-level work through a variety of student services.

Computer Skills: The computer lab has all of the equipment students need, including a digital camera, zip drives, scanners and more. A one-credit hour course for freshmen is available that provides detailed instruction in basic computer skills needed for college work.

Writing Support: The Writing Center gives free assistance to all undergrad and graduate students through peer tutors. Help is given at all steps of the process from writing an outline to final revisions. Tutoring is available on a walk-in and appointment basis.

Reading Skills: Reading instructors help students develop comprehension and vocabulary skills. They also show how to draw conclusions, make inference and recognize tone. A two-credit course called College Reading Skills is offered.

Study Skills: A two-credit course called Learning Strategies teaches note taking, time management, exam preparation and other study habits. Tutoring: Private (paid) tutors are available for students, and the college has a referral service to match tutors with students.

Supplemental Instruction: These sessions are free and led by students who have already completed the course. Students review lecture notes, clarify text materials, discuss ideas, organize material, evaluate and improve study skills and meet other students who are in the same class.

College Adjustment Program: These services are designed to help students who are struggling with the adjustment to college life. Services include free tutoring, academic advising and study skills instruction.

Ohio Northern University

Ada, OH

Address: 525 South Main Street, Ada, OH 45810
Phone: 419-772-2260
Admissions email: admissions-ug@onu.edu
Admissions contact: Karen Condeni, vice president and dean of enrollment
Website: www.onu.edu

Admissions Stats

Percentage of applicants admitted: 77.6%
Average GPA range: 3.4-3.5
SAT range: 520-620 verbal, 560-660 math
ACT range: 23-28 composite, 21-28 English, 23-28 math

Size

Number of undergraduates: 2,214

Costs

Tuition and fees: $25,815
Books and supplies: $900
On campus room and board and other expenses: $8,160
Off campus room and board and other expenses: $8,160

Academics

Majors offered: engineering, business, management, marketing and related support services, education, health professions and related clinical sciences, biological and biomedical sciences, arts and sciences, pharmacy, business administration and law

Favorite majors: engineering, business, management, marketing and related support services, education, health professions and related clinical sciences, biological and biomedical sciences

Student Life

The campus: ONU covers 285 acres but is in a city of only 5,000 people so it has a small-town atmosphere.

The students: The student population is 53% men and 47% women.

The B Features

Admission is based on class rank and SAT or ACT scores, but there is a strong willingness to look beyond the numbers. Letters of recommendation are not required but will be read if submitted. Extracurricular activities are considered, as well as recent academic trends. A special program helps with college transition.

Insight

This private liberal arts school is affiliated with United Methodist. According to Karen Condeni, vice president and dean of enrollment, the school makes a real effort to look past the standard statistics to the student behind them. "A strong number of students show potential but not number-wise," she says. "We look at their high school records overall as a whole picture and we look at trends." According to Condeni, the school also looks at personal information that might affect grades. "We look to see if students were working while going to school or if they had a single parent they had to help. We are looking for students who show determination.

"Ohio Northern University has a support program called College Transition that is not remedial work but helps students that need extra attention," says Condeni. For example, students in this program do not take a full load of classes (17 to 18 hours) but average 12 to 14 hours or three classes. "These students are monitored more closely and meet regularly with an advisor. Tutors are also available," she adds.

Ohio Wesleyan University

Delaware, OH

Address: 61 South Sandusky Street, Delaware, OH 43015-2370
Phone: 740-368-3020
Admissions email: awadmit@cc.owu.edu
Website: www.owu.edu

Admissions Stats

Percentage of applicants admitted: 73.7%
SAT range: 550-650 verbal, 550-660 math
ACT range: 24-28 composite, 23-29 English, 23-28 math

Size

Number of undergraduates: 568

Costs

Tuition and fees: $26,820
Books and supplies: $1,000
On campus room and board and other expenses: $8,380
Off campus room and board and other expenses: $6,250

Academics

Favorite majors: business, management, marketing and related support services, social sciences, psychology, biological and biomedical sciences, parks and recreation, leisure and fitness studies

The B Features

The Academic Skills Center's motto is "Improving the Student Inside You." It offers individual counseling that helps students assess their strengths and weaknesses and gives support in areas like time management, note taking, reading from texts, test taking and overcoming procrastination and anxiety. Group presentations are available on the same topics and may be given in fraternity houses, residence halls and other spots across the campus. A Lending Library gives students access to books on a variety of topics including coping with learning disabilities and developing study skills. Computerized assessments help identify individual specific study skill deficits.

In addition, the college offers a quantitative skills center that helps students gain confidence in their ability to do math and related subjects like astronomy, chemistry and economics.

Oregon State University

Corvallis, OR

Address: Office of Admissions, 104 Kerr Administration Building, Corvallis, OR 97331
Phone: 541-737-4411
Admissions email: osuadmit@orst.edu
Website: www.oregonstate.edu

Admissions Stats

Percentage of applicants admitted: 88.1%
SAT range: 470-590 verbal, 490-610 math
ACT range: 20-26 composite, 18-25 English, 19-26 math

Size

Number of undergraduates: 15,601

Costs

Tuition and fees: $5,319 in state, $17,667 out of state
Books and supplies: $1,350
On campus room and board and other expenses: $8,967
Off campus room and board and other expenses: $8,967

Academics

Favorite majors: business, management, marketing and related support services, biological and biomedical sciences, engineering, family and consumer sciences and human sciences, natural resources and conservation

The B Features

The College of Business Beta Alpha Psi is a co-ed professional accounting fraternity that sponsors an accounting library, provides resource materials and tutors accounting students.

The Center for Writing and Learning gives instructions and advice to students, including a study skills program. Basic writing skills such as organizing and revising are offered, and short grammar questions can be emailed in for assistance.

A student chapter offers tutoring in chemical engineering, and the chemistry department has a tutor list for an hourly fee. A general chemistry tutorial room known as the Mole Hole is available during certain weeks of each term.

Free tutoring is available for undergrads in lower division core economics courses and for students of electrical engineering and computer science. The department of ethnic studies offers mentoring for students of color or anyone else interested in changing social patterns of race, gender, ethnic, class and other issues.

The Department of Foreign Languages and Literatures has regular tutorial support for students taking French, German and Spanish.
The College of Forestry offers tutoring to students in forestry or related classes.

The Math Learning Center is available for drop-in tutoring help from undergrads and volunteers and multiple resources.
The Microbiology Student Association tutors students in that subject, and physics grad students offer help to students in introductory physics courses.

For students who have not yet declared a major, Exploratory Studies gives information, resources and other important materials to help.

Pine Manor College*

. . . .

Chestnut Hill, MA

Address: 400 Heath Street, Chestnut Hill, MA 02467
Phone: 617-731-7104
Admissions email: admissions@pmc.edu
Website: www.pmc.edu

Admissions Stats

Percentage of applicants admitted: 74.9%
SAT range: 360-480 verbal, 340-450 math
ACT range: 15-20 composite, 14-22 English, 14-19 math

Size

Number of undergraduates: 188

Costs

Tuition and fees: $14,544
Books and supplies: $956
On campus room and board and other expenses: $10,500
Off campus room and board and other expenses: $6,500

Academics

Favorite majors: business, management, marketing and related support services, communication, journalism and related programs, psychology, biological and biomedical services, visual and performing arts

---

The B Features

Freshmen are required to take a First Year Experience Seminar that is led by faculty members, student life professionals and peer mentors. During their second year, they take a Portfolio Learning Seminar. Its purpose is to "encourage students to become reflective, self-directed learners, as well as to help them understand and fulfill degree requirements through development of a personalized learning portfolio." Presentation of this portfolio is part of the requirements for graduation.

Many students use the Brown Learning Resource Center, staffed by professional, full-time tutors. Assistance is offered in writing, math, reading, study skills and time management. According to the college, at this resource center students are "able to discover previously untapped strengths, adjust to new demands of the college environment, fill gaps in prior learning and most of all, learn how to take charge of their own learning."

* All women college

Prescott College

Prescott, AZ

Address: 220 Grove Avenue, Prescott, AZ 86301
Phone: 1-877-350-2100
Admissions email: admissions@prescott.edu
Admissions contact: Natalie Canfield, admissions counselor
Website: www.prescott.edu

Admissions Stats

Percentage of applicants admitted: 85.2%
Average GPA range: 3.0
SAT range: Has not been required prior to Fall 2005
ACT range: Has not been required prior to Fall 2005

Size

Number of undergraduates: 500

Costs

Tuition and fees: $17,280
Books and supplies: $600
On campus room and board and other expenses: Not available
Off campus room and board and other expenses: $9,700

Academics

Favorite majors: environmental studies, creative writing, cultural and regional studies, and adventure education, therapeutic use of the wilderness, photography and counseling psychology

Student Life

The campus: This campus has a small, urban atmosphere and is close to the city of Prescott. It has a dozen buildings, including a library, café, classrooms and a community Crossroads Center. All buildings are within walking distance.

The students: 52% are women.

The B Features

Each student creates his/her own independent degree and then obtains faculty approval. The college strongly supports the individual and puts a heavy emphasis on hands-on learning with long, frequent off-campus trips. Classes have a cap of 12 students.

Insight

"We welcome students from a variety of backgrounds," says Natalie Canfield, admissions counselor. "We look at each person as a whole, not just numbers and essays. We look at bad grades and try to see how we can fix them." At Prescott, the essay is very evaluative for both writing level and content. The school requires two kinds of essays: one that is autobiographical ("To get to know the student") and one that is an academic autobiography ("To learn their writing style"). "Interviews are optional," continues Canfield. "They are relaxed and we talk about past education and different situations. We also give students a chance to ask us questions to see if we are a fit."

Prescott College focuses on degrees having to do with the environment. According to Canfield, it has more 15-passenger vans for field trips than it does buildings on campus. "Many courses are field based and most courses involve weekend-long trips," she explains.

SUNY College at Purchase

Purchase, NY

Address: 735 Anderson Hill Road, Purchase, NY 10577
Phone: 914-251-6300
Admissions email: admission@purchase.edu
Website: www.purchase.edu

Admissions Stats

Percentage of applicants admitted: 40.8%
SAT range: 520-620 verbal, 490-590 math
ACT range: Not available

Size

Number of undergraduates: 4,296

Costs

Tuition and fees: $4,350 in state, $10,610 out of state
Books and supplies: $2,200
On campus room and board and other expenses: $8,710
Off campus room and board and other expenses: $8,400

Academics

Favorite majors: visual and performing arts, liberal arts and sciences, general studies and humanities, social sciences, English language, literature/letters, communication, journalism and related programs

The B Features

Struggling students can go to the Learning Center for free tutoring services in writing, math and foreign languages. Tutors for additional subjects can be arranged. The center also offers students study skills help and printed materials in areas such as managing your time, making outlines, taking notes and studying. There are multimedia stations for computer assisted learning. Students interested in forming a study group can organize it through the Learning Center, and those with learning disabilities or other special needs can get help with a reading machine and other software.

Randolph-Macon College

Ashland, VA

Address: 204 Henry Street, Ashland, VA 23005-5505
Phone: 804-752-7305
Admissions email: admissions@rmc.edu
Website: www.rmc.edu

Admissions Stats

Percentage of applicants admitted: 77.2%
SAT range: 515-695 verbal, 520-640 math
ACT range: Not available

Size

Number of undergraduates: 1,100

Costs

Tuition and fees: $22,625
Books and supplies: $1,000
On campus room and board and other expenses: $8,010
Off campus room and board and other expenses: $4,110

Academics

Favorite majors: English language, literature/letters, psychology, biological and biomedical services, social sciences and history

The B Features

The Higgins Academic Center was named after Patrick John Higgins, an alumnus of Randolph-Macon. Because of his struggle with dyslexia, family and friends dedicated funds to open the center to help other students with various learning disabilities. The center offers tutoring and mentoring services as well as academic support and pays special attention to students' various learning styles.

University of Redlands

Redlands, CA

Address: 1200 East Colton Avenue, P.O. Box 3080, Redlands, CA 92373-0999
Phone: 800-455-5064
Admissions email: admissions@uor.edu
Website: www.redlands.edu

Admissions Stats

Percentage of applicants admitted: 70.8%
SAT range: 530-620 verbal, 530-620 math
ACT range: 22-27 composite

Size

Number of undergraduates: 3,206

Costs

Tuition and fees: $25,524
Books and supplies: $1,000
On campus room and board and other expenses: $10,990
Off campus room and board and other expenses: $10,635

Academics

Favorite majors: business, management, marketing and related support services, visual and performing arts, social sciences, liberal arts and sciences, health professions and related clinical services, general studies and humanities

The B Features

Academic Support Services helps students develop and strengthen the skills they will need most for academic success. It does this through academic counseling, subject tutoring, writing tutoring and a Learning Skills course. With academic counseling, students are encouraged to talk to their advisors about choosing a major, planning for possible study abroad and learning time management and study skills. The tutoring center provides time management calendars, study skills handouts and other materials.

The Learning Skills course is offered each semester and covers time management, improving memory, understanding learning styles and developing positive attitudes and motivation. Time is spent discussing goal setting, career planning, test taking and note taking. Redlands also offers free peer tutoring, and students are allowed two hours per week, unless they have a documented learning disability. Writing tutors can be accessed on a drop-in basis and can help with all stages of writing from outlining to footnoting.

University of Rhode Island

Kingston, RI

Address: Undergraduate Admissions Office, 14 Upper College Road, Kingston, RI 02881
Phone: 401-874-7000
Admissions email: uriadmit@etal.uri.edu
Website: www.uri.edu

Admissions Stats

Percentage of applicants admitted: 70.6%
SAT range: 490-590 verbal, 500-600 math
ACT range: Not available

Size

Number of undergraduates: 11,298

Costs

Tuition and fees: $6,752 in state, $18,338 out of state
Books and supplies: $800
On campus room and board and other expenses: $9,560
Off campus room and board and other expenses: $10,092

Academics

Favorite majors: business, management, marketing and related support services, communication, journalism and related programs, family and consumer sciences, human sciences and engineering

---

The B Features

The Academic Enhancement Center's motto is "Teaching Is Learning." This reflects its belief that "learning happens best when the learner is engaged in teaching subject matter to others." Students are helped through peer tutoring and study groups on set classes and general study skills topics. The online assistance center has excellent materials to be read and/or downloaded.

The college advocates study groups that get together once a week and share responsibility for the material they are all learning. They are encouraged to discuss class materials, work together to solve problems, compare notes and help each other to succeed.

The URI Writing Center is free to all students who need help with all levels of writing.

Rider University

Lawrenceville, NJ

Address: 2083 Lawrence Road, Lawrenceville, NJ 08648-3099
Phone: 609-896-5042
Admissions email: admissions@rider.edu
Website: www.rider.edu

Admissions Stats

Percentage of applicants admitted: 78.4%
SAT range: 470-560 verbal, 480-580 math
ACT range: Not available

Size

Number of undergraduates: 4,329

Costs

Tuition and fees: $22,500
Books and supplies: $1,000
On campus room and board and other expenses: $10,400
Off campus room and board and other expenses: $10,400

Academics

Favorite majors: psychology, business, management, marketing and related support services, English language, literature/letters, education, computer and information sciences and support services

---
The B Features

Tutoring services are available through the Rider Learning Center by peer tutors who have gotten excellent grades in the courses they work with and are recommended by professors. Tutors work on both a drop-in and appointment basis. The center also offers a math skills lab.

Rider offers supplemental instruction for the most difficult classes. In this, students review notes, go over readings and learn test-taking strategies. Rider has two core classes for first-year students who have not met the criteria for college level reading: Introduction to Academic Reading and College Reading.

In the first class, which is required, reading and learning strategies are taught to help students increase their reading comprehension. This class earns two credits. In the second (elective) course, students earn three credits by developing and improving reading comprehension skills and study strategies.

Rust College
· ·

Holly Springs, MO

Address: 1500 Rust Avenue, Holly Springs, MO 38535
Phone: 662-252-8000 ext. 4059
Website: www.rustcollege.edu

Admissions Stats

SAT range: Open admissions
ACT range: Open admissions

Size

Number of undergraduates: 254

Costs

Tuition and fees: $8,600
Books and supplies: $500
On campus room and board and other expenses: $4,100
Off campus room and board and other expenses: $5,100

Academics

Favorite majors: computer and information sciences and support services, business, management, marketing and related support services, social sciences, biological and biomedical services and English language and literature/letters

The B Features

With its open admissions system, the college considers students whose "educational goals, career objectives and intellectual abilities match the institution's academic and non-academic programs." The Academic Counseling Program helps students plan based on needs and interests. Freshmen are assigned faculty advisors. After the first year, a major is declared, and each student has an academic counselor from the faculty to help with any problems or questions.

Saint John's University

Collegeville, MN

Address: P.O. Box 2000, Collegeville, MN 56321
Phone: 320-363-2196
Admissions email: admissions@csbsju.edu
Website: www.csbsju.edu

Admissions Stats

Percentage of applicants admitted: 86%
SAT range: 520-640 verbal, 560-660 math
ACT range: 23-28 composite, 22-27 English, 23-28 math

Size

Number of undergraduates: 1,940

Costs

Tuition and fees: $22,148
Books and supplies: $800
On campus room and board and other expenses: $7,017
Off campus room and board and other expenses: $7,017

Academics

Favorite majors: business, management, marketing and related support services, social sciences, psychology, English language and literature/letters and biological and biomedical sciences

---
The B Features

The Writing Center works through drop in and appointment. The Math Skills Center helps students with all 100-level math classes as well as preparing for the math proficiency exam, reviewing algebra, geometry, trigonometry and pre-calculus, working on assignments for math classes and preparing for the math portions of standardized tests. In addition, the college offers an Academic Skills Center Reading Lab.

Salve Regina University

· ·

Newport, RI

Address: 100 Ochre Point Avenue, Newport, RI 02840
Phone: 401-341-2908
Admissions email: sruadmis@salve.edu
Admissions contact: Amanda (Mandy) Warhurst Webster, senior associate director of admissions
Website: www.salve.edu

Admissions Stats

Percentage of applicants admitted: 56.2%
Average GPA range: 2.7-3.7
SAT range: 1030-1100 combined, 500-590 verbal, 500-570 math
ACT range: 22-26 composite, 20-27 English, 20-26 math

Size

Number of undergraduates: 2,069

Costs

Tuition and fees: $23,500
Books and supplies: $800
On campus room and board and other expenses: $10,000
Off campus room and board and other expenses: $7,500
Degrees offered: doctor's, master's, bachelor's and associate's degrees

---
Academics

Favorite majors: business, management, marketing and related support services, education, security and protective services, English language and literature/letters, psychology

---
Student Life

The campus: Covering 79 acres, the campus has 44 buildings and is on the oceanfront in the mansion district of Newport, the Sailing Capital of the World. It is 10 minutes from the Newport beaches. Most of the buildings on campus are mansions themselves and considered "architecturally significant." The atmosphere is very New England and a great deal of restoration has been done on the Vanderbilt and other mansions on the grounds. Imported trees from all over the world are found on campus grounds.

The students: Three-quarters come from New England and the mid-Atlantic states. Although the college was founded in 1934 by the Sisters of Mercy, students do not have to be Catholic to attend the school.

The B Features

Salve Regina looks at a student's high school transcript, and one of the first things it does is recalculate the GPA. All extracurricular classes are eliminated and the average is obtained from the core academic classes only. A Writing Center and Student Tutorial Center are offered, and the faculty and staff make an extra effort to help first-year students with the transition.

Insight

"There is a college for everyone," says Amanda Warhurst Webster, senior associate director of admissions. "Here we look at the profile of the high school itself. Does it offer an honors curriculum? How many academic classes will the student choose to take, including in their senior year? Do the students take state tests?" According to Warhurst Webster, emphasis is also put on recommendations. "We want to see the third party perspective," she says. "And we can tell when a letter is a general one or a truly personal one."

The essay is very important at Salve Regina. "It is the only part of the application process that is in the student's own voice," says Warhurst Webster. "The essays bring the kids to life. I always encourage students to think, 'How do I want to appear to the people in admissions?'" The essay topics are open-ended, and officers look at the concepts presented in the essay along with grammar, mechanics and usage issues. One common essay example is "Tell us something more about yourself that you want us to know."

"We certainly give leeway to students who do not have a support system," explains Warhurst Webster.

University of San Francisco

San Francisco, CA

Address: 2130 Fulton Street, San Francisco, CA 94117-1080
Phone: 415-422-6563
Admissions email: admission@usfca.edu
Website: www.usfca.edu

Admissions Stats

Percentage of applicants admitted: 74.2%
SAT range: 500-610 verbal, 500-610 math
ACT range: 21-26

Size

Number of undergraduates: 4,718

Costs

Tuition and fees: $24,800
Books and supplies: $900
On campus room and board and other expenses: $12,980
Off campus room and board and other expenses: $13,200

Academics

Favorite majors: psychology, business, management, marketing and related support services social sciences, communication, journalism and related programs, computer information sciences and support services

---

The B Features

The Learning Center helps students through tutors in a variety of academic disciplines. The tutors are undergrads and graduate students who have excelled in that area and have had special training. They cover such topics as math, science, business, languages, computers, arts and general education. Study skills videos, textbooks and reference books are available, and the center also provides students a place to study that is peaceful and supportive. The Writing Center features tutors that tailor programs of instruction to meet each student's needs. Its primary goal is to "guide students in developing their writing skills in rhetoric, style and correctness, through one-on-one interactive conferences with Rhetoric and Composition faculty who have been chosen to work as consultants."

Schreiner University

Kerrville, TX

Address: 2100 Memorial Boulevard, Kerrville, TX 78028
Phone: 800-343-4919
Admissions email: admissions@schreiner.edu
Admissions contact: Sandra Speed, dean of admission and financial aid
Website: www.schreiner.edu

Admissions Stats

Percentage of applicants admitted: 65%
Average GPA range: 3.46
SAT range: 460-570 verbal, 470-560 math; 1013 average SAT score
ACT range: 19-25 composite, 18-25 English, 18-25 math; 22 average ACT

Size

Number of undergraduates: 737

Costs

Tuition and fees: $15,142
Books and supplies: $1,000
On campus room and board and other expenses: $8,615
Off campus room and board and other expenses: $6,520

Academics

Favorite majors: business administration, life sciences, teacher education, exercise science

Student Life

The campus: About an hour northwest of San Antonio, this small, liberal arts, private college affiliated with the Presbyterian Church (USA) is in Kerrville, a city of 20,000. There are four residence halls and one apartment complex on campus. The campus has wireless hotspots in nearly every area, and a modern activity center is where students go to hang out, play pool, listen to music, have a snack, work out in the fitness center or relax by the fireplace. The campus is located on the banks of the Guadalupe River and is home to an abundance of gentle wildlife including a flock of whitetail deer.

The students: Most students live on campus and enjoy the traditional residential lifestyle. Nearly a quarter of Schreiner's undergraduates participate in NCAA Division III athletics. There are slightly more women than men at Schreiner and almost a quarter of the population is minority.

The B Features

Students with learning disabilities will find help through the Learning Support Services Program. The student to faculty ratio is 13:1, you can help design your own internship and tutoring for all classes is free. There is also a strong honors program at Schreiner.

Insight

Sandra Speed, dean of admission and financial aid, has important information for anyone thinking about coming to Schreiner. "If you want to fall through the cracks, do not come here," she warns. "If you don't come to class, you will be missed, and someone will try to help you resolve the problem before it becomes a bigger issue. The faculty at Schreiner is very involved with each student's success. They have a real personal commitment to students and will even give you their home phone numbers. At Schreiner, counseling is consistent and ongoing." The school has a faith-based mission and a strong emphasis on extracurricular work within the community, school and church.

A student, Jay Govan III, took time to explain why he chose Schreiner University. "What led me to Schreiner was the ratio of students to professors," he explains. "I knew that would be a great benefit to me because if I were to struggle the teachers always have their doors open to students and help. What also led me to this school was the tutoring they have, which is great."

Govan's freshman and sophomore years of high school were at Trinity Christian Academy, a very small school, and he believes that is where he learned to be responsible in getting his work done on time. His junior and senior years were at Saint Anthony's Catholic High School, an all-boys school. He admits he was not looking forward to attending the school at first, but he says, "after a couple of weeks things started going well. The good thing about an all-boys school is that you don't have to try to impress anyone but just worry about getting your studies done. While I was a senior there, my grades were good enough to allow me to also take a couple of college courses at the University of the Incarnate Word."

During his first year at Schreiner, Govan's GPA dropped from 3.0 to 2.5, an issue he is keenly aware of. "I have been working hard to continue to increase it to where it was in high school," he says. "The teachers are always persuading me to give it all I have and not hold anything back."

Govan has suggestions for students thinking about attending Schreiner. "This is a great school to come to and be focused on your books and not get sidetracked like if you went to a college in a big city. I would also encourage students to get all the education you can get now because after school is over that's it, it's time to go out and look for a job, and no more thinking about skipping or being late."

He has learned some important things at college already. "You have to make goals for yourself and make studying and class your number one priority," he advises.

Shaw University

Raleigh, NC

Address: 118 East South Street, Raleigh, NC 27601
Phone: 919-546-8275
Website: www.shawu.edu

Admissions Stats

Percentage of applicants admitted: 44.3%
SAT range: 330-430 verbal, 315-445 math
ACT range: 13-17 composite

Size

Number of undergraduates: 2,446

Costs

Tuition and fees: $9,438
Books and supplies: $700
On campus room and board and other expenses: $7,550
Off campus room and board and other expenses: $7,550

Academics

Favorite majors: business, management, marketing and related support services, security and protective services, public administration and social service professions, social sciences, philosophy and religious studies

The B Features

The Freshman Year Program is focused on providing the tools students need to reach their academic goals. It features a series of activities and events that help students become more familiar with college life and ease the transition. Every student must take this program as part of graduation requirements. It includes a number of classes, including a cultural and spiritual enrichment seminar.

Note that the college has a dress code, and community worship is mandatory, as is attendance to college events such as Homecoming, Senior Appreciation Day and University Awards Day.

A new, free program called Freshmen Academy earns credit hours. It is an intense summer academic program, and participants receive room, board, books and supplies. They attend workshops, seminars, field trips and presentations.

Simmons College*

Boston, MA

Address: 300 The Fenway, Boston, MA 02115
Phone: 617-521-8468
Admissions email: ugadm@simmons.edu
Website: www.simmons.edu

Admissions Stats

Percentage of applicants admitted: 67.3%
SAT range: 510-610 verbal, 500-590 math
ACT range: 21-25 composite

Size

Number of undergraduates: 1,555

Costs

Tuition and fees: $24,490
Books and supplies: $800
On campus room and board and other expenses: $12,030
Off campus room and board and other expenses: $12,030

Academics

Favorite majors: social sciences, health professions and related clinical services, communication, journalism and related programs, psychology, visual and performing arts

The B Features

Simmon's Academic Support Center is focused on providing high-quality assistance to help students succeed academically. According to the college, its goal is to "help students become independent learners and to encourage them to take an active part in their educational and intellectual pursuits." The center achieves this through various methods.

Academic Advising and Counseling assigns advisors to students who are having academic struggles. Placement examinations are given and provide results for math, language and chemistry levels. Services for Students with Disabilities is for those with a documented disability, while Tutorial Services matches students with course tutors in such subjects as biology, chemistry, foreign languages, math and physics. There are also study groups with weekly reviews of course material. Specialists offer one-on-one help by appointment and give instruction on study skills. Writing Assistance provides coaches to help students organize and structure their writing and learn how to self-edit.

* All women college

Sonoma State University

. . . .

Rohnert Park, CA

Address: 1801 East Cotati Avenue, Rohnert Park, CA 94928-3609
Phone: 707-664-2326
Admissions email: admitme@sonoma.edu
Website: www.sonoma.edu

Admissions Stats

Percentage of applicants admitted: 79.9%
SAT range: verbal 460-560, math 460-560
ACT range: Not available

Size

Number of undergraduates: 7,123

Costs

Tuition and fees: $3,408 in state, $13,578 out of state
Books and supplies: $1,260
On campus room and board and other expenses: $11,469
Off campus room and board and other expenses: $13,014

Academics

Favorite majors: business, management, marketing and related support services, engineering, computer and informational sciences and support services, health professions and related clinical sciences, visual and performing arts

---

The B Features

An Educational Mentoring Team helps students keep up with college life through a Freshman Seminar and a strong advising department. They feel students should be connected to a faculty member, a student services professional and a peer mentor.

The Freshman Seminar is an optional class, but all new students are encouraged to take it. It focuses on expanding the skills needed to succeed in classes, discusses the university culture, provides individualized advising and helps students to increase their involvement in their own education. SOAR, or Sonoma Orientation, Advising and Registration, is held each summer for entering freshmen and their parents and is geared to help with the transition to college life.

Free tutoring is available for all undergraduate courses. Students are allowed four hours a week, with a maximum of two hours per subject.

Spelman College*

. . . .

Atlanta, GA

Address: 350 Spelman Lane Southwest, Atlanta, GA 30314-4399
Phone: 404-270-5193
Admissions email: admissions@spelman.edu
Website: www.spelman.edu

Admissions Stats

Percentage of applicants admitted: 38.9%
SAT range: 500-580 verbal, 490-580 math
ACT range: 20-24 composite

Size

Number of undergraduates: 496

Costs

Tuition and fees: $15,190
Books and supplies: $1,658
On campus room and board and other expenses: $11,390
Off campus room and board and other expenses: $11,390

Academics

Favorite majors: English language and literature/letters, psychology, biological and biomedical sciences, social sciences, computer and information sciences and support services

The B Features

The Learning Resources Center is where students go for extra help. It is open to all students and offers services such as lab instruction, academic advisement, peer tutoring, workshops and instruction in study techniques and learning strategies. According to the college, the center's major objective is to "EMPOWER students who will become creative, independent learners and problem solvers capable of processing and handling volumes of information."

Student Success Workshops are offered in areas such as Getting Motivated and How to Calculate Your GPA and Stay Informed. Peer tutors are available on both a drop in and appointment basis throughout the year. Students can get help in study techniques, reading, note taking, test-taking strategies, problem solving and communication skills. Academic advising is also offered through the Learning Resources Center.

* Historically Black college for women

Suffolk University

Boston, MA

Address: 8 Ashburton Place, Beacon Hill, Boston, MA 02108
Phone: 617-573-8460
Admissions email: admissions@suffolk.edu
Website: www.suffolk.edu

Admissions Stats

Percentage of applicants admitted: 85%
SAT range: 540-550 verbal, 450-550 math
ACT range: Not available

Size

Number of undergraduates: 4,181

Costs

Tuition and fees: $19,790
Books and supplies: $1,000
On campus room and board and other expenses: $14,516
Off campus room and board and other expenses: $13,822

Academics

Favorite majors: psychology, business, management, marketing and related support services, visual and performing arts, social sciences, communication, and journalism and related programs

The B Features

Suffolk has many different methods of helping students who are feeling a little lost or falling behind. At the Ballotti Learning Center, a Tutor Program matches students with peer tutors that can either help in the course that is proving difficult or teach general academic strategies like note taking, exam prep, time management, etc. The service is free, and tutors and students meet up to twice a week for one-hour sessions. In a survey done by the Learning Center, 97 percent of the students tutored reported feeling that tutoring helped them to become more independent learners. Study groups are also offered at the center. They focus on the traditionally high-risk courses and give students the time to review notes and prepare questions for class.

The staff consultants at Ballotti are doctoral students in psychology and assist students with personal concerns and challenges. (Sessions are private and confidential.)

The AHANA (African Hispanic Asian Native American) International Program is an outreach program for students of color. Peer liaisons help with issues like second language, stereotypes and cultural differences that may occur.

Suffolk's High Profile Program is for students who are in "academic jeopardy." A team of counselors and technicians connect these students with services that could help academically. The Roster Project identifies students who are heading for "academic risk" by mid- semester (at risk of failing because of missing class, poor study habits or communication skills, second language issues, etc.). Letters or calls are made as a warning and then students are encouraged to seek the help they need.

Educational consultants are on campus to address issues that affect a student's academic life. This often includes matching student with tutor and then monitoring the relationship to make sure it is successful and effective.

Sweet Briar College*

Sweet Briar, VA

Address: 134 Chapel Drive, Sweet Briar, VA 24595-9998
Phone: 434-381-6142
Admissions email: admissions@sbc.edu
Website: www.sbc.edu

Admissions Stats

Percentage of applicants admitted: 79.4%
Average GPA range: 27% in top 10% of high school class
SAT range: 530-648 verbal, 500-608 math
ACT range: 23-28 composite, 22-28 English, 19-26 math

Size

Number of undergraduates: 700

Costs

Tuition and fees: $20,880
Books and supplies: $600
On campus room and board and other expenses: $9,870
Off campus room and board and other expenses: $6,750

Academics

Favorite majors: English language, literature/letters, psychology, visual and performing arts, social sciences, foreign languages, literatures and linguistics

The B Features

The Academic Resource Center is full of different ways to help make college life and courses easier. It is available to all students and is staffed by trained student assistants. ARC offers information on time management, writing, reading, study skills, stress management, peer tutoring and mentoring, assistance for learning differences and focuses on "encouraging a higher standard of academic performance." The writing tutoring service is ARC's main focus. The staff works with students on all stages from forming a thesis to perfecting punctuation. Experienced student mentors help freshmen adjust to college academics.

ARC also offers online and printed resources on topics like Creating a Weekly Time Management Schedule or Anticipating and Planning for Courses. In addition, ARC assists with the social aspects of college life and the potential stress it can bring through Stress Management Training.

* All women college

Temple University

. . . .

Philadelphia, PA

Address: Temple University, 1801 N. Broad Street, Philadelphia, PA 19122-6096
Phone: 215-304-7200
Admissions email: tuadm@mail.temple.edu
Website: www.temple.edu

Admissions Stats

Percentage of applicants admitted: 60%
SAT range: 490-590 verbal, 490-590 math
ACT range: Not available

Size

Number of undergraduates: 22,215

Costs

Tuition and fees: $9,102 in state, $16,268 out of state
Books and supplies: $800
On campus room and board and other expenses: $11,638
Off campus room and board and other expenses: $11,064

Academics

Favorite majors: psychology, business, management, marketing and related support services, visual and performing arts, communication, journalism and related programs

The B Features

Keeping up with computer needs is not a problem with more than 30 computer labs on campus plus a Student Computer Center. The college has a range of professional academic advisors to aid students with choosing majors and resolving academic issues. The advising center offers a new student orientation, curriculum advising and "academic counseling for students to develop a meaningful education plan compatible with life goals."

The Student Support Services Program is part of the Russell Conwell Educational Service Center. It gives students intensive academic support through free year round counseling and tutoring activities. In addition, the college offers a required six-week intensive Summer Bridge Program that includes skill building courses in math, computer technology, library usage, reading, writing and study skills as well as workshops on personal development, art appreciation and career choices. The tutorial component of the learning center is based on tutoring sessions in selected subjects, while the counseling component provides academic, career and personal counseling

University of Tennessee

Knoxville, TN

Address: Circle Park, Knoxville, TN 37996
Phone: 865-974-2184
Admissions email: admissions@tennessee.edu
Website: www.tennessee.edu

Admissions Stats

Percentage of applicants admitted: 44.2%
SAT range: 500-610 verbal, 500-620 math
ACT range: 21-26 composite, 21-28 English, 20-26 math

Size

Number of undergraduates: 19,224

Costs

Tuition and fees: $4,748 in state, $14,528 out of state
Books and supplies: $1,156
On campus room and board and other expenses: $10,002
Off campus room and board and other expenses: $9,400

Academics

Favorite majors: business, management, marketing and related support services, social sciences, psychology, communication, journalism and related programs and engineering

The B Features

The Student Academic Support Services is centered on promoting student progress. Services are free and confidential. Help is given in time management, test taking, reading efficiency, note taking and use, information retention and learning organization. The SASS library has materials on learning strategies, review books, a 12-station computer lab and an audio-visual room that has videos and tapes on study skill issues. Workshops on specific study skills are available each semester as well.

SASS offers individual meetings with educational specialists for consultation or coaching. Students can also be assessed to discover their learning strengths and weaknesses. A Teaching Style Inventory and a Test Anxiety Inventory are available. Skill-specific labs are offered each semester on critical thinking, verbal and communication skills, vocabulary, grammar and reading rate and comprehension. A Learning Resources Library provides practice questions and other reference material to check out.

Thiel College

Greenville, PA

Address: 75 College Avenue, Greenville, PA 16125
Phone: 724-589-2345
Admissions email: admission@thiel.edu
Website: www.thiel.edu

Admissions Stats

Percentage of applicants admitted: 78.8%
SAT range: 420-530 verbal, 420-533 math
ACT range: 18-22 composite, 15-23 English, 17-23 math

Size

Number of undergraduates: 404

Costs

Tuition and fees: $15,990
Books and supplies: $700
On campus room and board and other expenses: $8,514
Off campus room and board and other expenses: $8,890

Academics

Favorite majors: business, management, marketing and related support services, psychology, social sciences, security and protective services, biological and biomedical services

The B Features

Thiel's Academic Services Center offers study skills courses, tutoring, study groups, reading and writing programs, testing and help with achieving academic goals. One of the center's services is supplemental instruction. Student leaders go to class with students and then conduct review sessions three times a week for the duration of the semester. These sessions are optional and involve discussion, supplemental worksheets and practice tests.

A one-credit course called Freshmen Study Skills GEN 001 is designed to enhance students' ability for critical thinking and learning academic success strategies. "We will investigate campus resources, learning styles, educational goals and career goals," the college says.

Tutoring is free for all students and is given in most subject areas from both peer and professional tutors and in both individual and study group sessions. A Writing Lab is available for students needing help with grammar or other steps in writing college papers.

Tuskegee University

Tuskegee, AL

Address: Kresge Center, 3rd floor, Tuskegee, AL 36008-1920
Phone: 334-727-8500
Admissions email: admi@tuskegee.edu
Website: www.tuskegee.edu

Admissions Stats

Percentage of applicants admitted: 80.5%
SAT range: 340-540 verbal, 370-550 math
ACT range: Not available

Size

Number of undergraduates: 2,391

Costs

Tuition and fees: $11,590
Books and supplies: $873
On campus room and board and other expenses: $8,456
Off campus room and board and other expenses: $7,765

Academics

Favorite majors: psychology, business, management, marketing and related support services, biological/biomedical sciences, engineering, agriculture, agriculture operations and related sciences

The B Features

A predominantly African American college (76.1%), Tuskegee offers a peer tutoring program for students who are taking first- or second-year courses in gross anatomy, microanatomy, neuroanatomy, physiology, microbiology, parasitology or clinical pathology, anatomic pathology and pharmacology. Peer tutors also are available to help the needs of nursing, medical technology and occupational therapy students. These tutors give advice and guidance on lectures, monitor questioning and answering skills and help establish study groups.

An Academic Skills Guide discusses the importance of effective study skills. According to the college, the guide "addresses the how-to's of studying" and covers such elements as taking part in effective group study, developing thinking skills, taking tests and notes and managing time.

University of Utah

. . . .

Salt Lake City, UT

Address: 201 Presidents Circle, Salt Lake City, UT 84112-9008
Phone: 801-581-7281
Admissions email: admissions@sa.utah.edu
Website: www.utah.edu

Admissions Stats

Percentage of applicants admitted: 86.4%
SAT range: Not available
ACT range: 21-26 composite, 20-26 English, 19-26 math

Size

Number of undergraduates: 22,421

Costs

Tuition and fees: $4,000 in state, $12,410 out of state
Books and supplies: $1,086
On campus room and board and other expenses: $9,096
Off campus room and board and other expenses: $9,634

Academics

Favorite majors: business, management, marketing and related support services, visual and performing arts, social science, communication, journalism and related programs, engineering

---

The B Features

Students can turn to PASS, or Programs for Academic Support, for help. Through PASS, students can get free peer tutoring in physics, chemistry, science, some foreign languages and math, either one on one or in a group. Online tutoring has recently been expanded. A Self-Help Learning Lab features audio and videotapes, books and computer software for help in study skills, reading, algebra, calculus, trigonometry, statistics, differential equations, chemistry and foreign language.

Academic advising is available in study skills and time management, effective listening and note taking, improving reading comprehension, test taking, test anxiety and knowing your learning style. Supplemental instruction is provided for the historically difficult entry level classes.

Washington State University

Pullman, WA

Address: French Administration Building, Pullman, WA 99164-1009
Phone: 509-335-5586
Admissions email: admiss2@wsu.edu
Website: www.wsu.edu

Admissions Stats

Percentage of applicants admitted: 75.3%
SAT range: 470-580 verbal, 490-600 math
ACT range: 19-25 composite

Size

Number of undergraduates: 18,746

Costs

Tuition and fees: $5,628 in state, $14,046 out of state
Books and supplies: $912
On campus room and board and other expenses: $9,912
Off campus room and board and other expenses: $12,200

Academics

Favorite majors: business, management, marketing and related support services, social sciences, communication, journalism and related programs, education and engineering

---

The B Features

Students go to the SALC, or Student Advising and Learning Center, for academic assistance. This provides advising, tutoring and other help. Academic Assistance offers services such as learning-strategies workshops, handouts, videos and a peer tutorial program for one-on-one assistance in a wide range of subjects for an hourly fee.

A two-credit elective class called the Freshman Seminar is designed to "help first-year students enhance critical thinking, research, writing and presentation skills as well as deal with transition issues faced when entering into the university." Students enrolled in this class develop a research project about the lessons learned in the course.

Wells College

Aurora, NY

Address: 176 State Route 90, Aurora, NY 13026-0500
Phone: 315-364-3264
Admissions email: admissions@wells.edu
Website: www.wells.edu

Admissions Stats

Percentage of applicants admitted: 77%
SAT range: 510-640 verbal, 490-610 math
ACT range: 21-27

Size

Number of undergraduates: 450

Costs

Tuition and fees: $14,900
Books and supplies: $700
On campus room and board and other expenses: $7,700
Off campus room and board and other expenses: $9,700

Academics

Favorite majors: English language literature/letters, psychology, visual and performing arts, biological/biomedical sciences, social sciences

---

The B Features

The First Year Experience (WLLS 101) is required and designed to acquaint freshmen with the four divisions of social sciences, humanities, sciences and fine arts and their connection to liberal arts. The class helps students to think, read and write critically, discuss complex issues, communicate effectively, use college resources precisely and learn as a group. It is taught in a combination of discussion and workshop.

Wesleyan College*

Macon, GA

Address: 4760 Forsyth Road, Macon, GA 31210
Phone: 478-757-5206
Admissions email: admissions@wesleyancollege.edu
Website: www.wesleyancollege.edu

Admissions Stats

Percentage of applicants admitted: 54.8%
SAT range: 490-610 verbal, 470-590 math
ACT range: 20-25 composite, 19-25 English, 18-23 math

Size

Number of undergraduates: 661

Costs

Tuition and fees: $10,900
Books and supplies: $800
On campus room and board and other expenses: $8,950
Off campus room and board and other expenses: $8,950

Academics

Favorite majors: business, management, marketing and related support services, psychology, communication, journalism and related programs, visual and performing arts, biological and biomedical services

The B Features

Student-to-faculty ratio is 11:1, and class sizes are 19 and under. Wesleyan is billed as the oldest college for women in the world. The school offers an Academic Center that provides free tutoring and counseling for students who may be struggling in their classes. Group and individual sessions are available year round, either by appointment or as a drop in.

* All women college

Westminster College

New Wilmington, PA

Address: 319 South Market Street, New Wilmington, PA 16172
Phone: 724-946-7100
Admissions email: admis@westminster.edu
Website: www.westminster.edu

Admissions Stats

Percentage of applicants admitted: 75.4%
SAT range: 490-590 verbal, 480-600 math
ACT range: 20-26 composite, 19-26 English, 19-26 math

Size

Number of undergraduates: 1,576

Costs

Tuition and fees: $20,530
Books and supplies: $1,700
On campus room and board and other expenses: $6,860
Off campus room and board and other expenses: $6,690

Academics

Favorite majors: education, business, management, marketing and related support services, social sciences, communication, journalism and related programs and biological and biomedical services

---

The B Features

The Westminster Plan provides a complete core curriculum in science, humanities, math, computer science and religion (it is Presbyterian based). All students graduate with two majors. Student-to-faculty ratio is 13:1, and most classes are no more than 19 students. The school emphasizes that it takes education seriously and that this is not a "party school."

West Virginia University

Morgantown, WV

Address: President's Office, Box 6201, Morgantown, WV 26506-6201
Phone: 800-344-9881
Admissions email: wuadmissions@arc.wvu.edu
Website: www.wvu.edu

Admissions Stats

Percentage of applicants admitted: 92.4%
SAT range: 480-570 verbal, 480-580 math
ACT range: 20-25 composite, 20-26 English, 18-25 math

Size

Number of undergraduates: 17,517

Costs

Tuition and fees: $3,938 in state, $12,060 out of state
Books and supplies: $800
On campus room and board and other expenses: $8,448
Off campus room and board and other expenses: $8,314

Academics

Favorite majors: business, management, marketing and related support services, social sciences, communication, journalism and related programs, engineering, liberal arts and sciences, general studies and humanities

The B Features

With almost 4,000 freshmen entering WVU each year, a large program is required to support them academically. Enter University 101, a class geared to help freshmen adjust to university life and its demands. A passing grade in this course is required for graduation. In the fall semester, students also may take the SSS Orientation Course, which is designed to orient them to academic requirements and how student support services can help.

In assigning residence halls, the college places freshmen with similar majors and/or passions in the same dorm, enabling them to form peer study groups and meet others with the same interests. WVU offers its students a math lab through its Learning Center. Anyone needing help with writing skills can attend sessions geared to help with everything from letters to research papers. Students who are still not sure about their major can get assistance through the Student Support Services professional staff of advisors. Free tutoring is available for most general classes in either one-on-one or study group sessions.

Whittier College

Address: 13406 East Philadelphia Street, Whittier, CA 90608
Phone: 562-907-4238
Admissions email: admissions@whittier.edu
Website: www.whittier.edu

Admissions Stats

Percentage of applicants admitted: 79.3%
SAT range: 480-590 verbal, 470-590 math
ACT range: 19-25 composite

Size

Number of undergraduates: 1,203

Costs

Tuition and fees: $24,468
Books and supplies: $656
On campus room and board and other expenses: $9,662
Off campus room and board and other expenses: $8,084

Academics

Favorite majors: English language, literature/letters, psychology, business, management, marketing and related support services, biological and biomedical sciences, social sciences

The B Features

At Whittier's Center for Academic Success, tutoring is free and classes that have been identified as historically challenging for most students are supported through supplemental instruction. Group sessions review notes, practice quizzes and work to reinforce the knowledge and skills they need for the class.

CAS also offers a class called Succeeding in College that helps students find out how to do well in school, both academically and personally. The class features individual exercises, cooperative learning, reading and lectures and is available each spring. Students that need assistance in the writing process can find all the help they need through the Writing Program.

Wilkes University

. . . . .

Wilkes-Barre, PA

Address: 84 West South Street, Wilkes-Barre, PA 18766
Phone: 1-800-WILKES-U
Admissions email: admissions@wilkes.edu
Admissions contact: Mike Frantz, vice president of enrollment and marketing
Website: www.wilkes.edu

Admissions Stats

Average GPA: 3.3
SAT range: 450-590 verbal, 490-620 math

Size

Number of undergraduates: 2,350

Costs

Tuition and fees: $21,646
Books and supplies: $1,050
On campus room and board and other expenses: $9,720
Off campus room and board and other expenses: $7,400

Academics

Majors offered: The school focuses on pre-professional preparation especially in the health sciences and has the only doctorate in pharmacy in the region through the Nesbitt School of Pharmacy.

The B Features

Wilkes has a deep interest in helping the B student achieve excellence through a dedicated faculty and personal tutoring. Admissions are based on secondary-school record, class rank and results of the SAT or ACT. Interviews are not required but highly recommended. Essays and letters of recommendation are not required but will be accepted and considered if submitted.

Student Life

The campus: The 27-acre campus is nestled within historic Wilkes-Barre, right next to the beautiful Susquehanna River. Each of the 24 resident halls is unique and range from stately mansions, to contemporary dorms, to brick Tudor mansions. The campus is fast becoming pedestrian friendly with eight academic buildings, eight administrative buildings, a library, faculty and alumni house, art gallery, bell tower, an athletic sports complex and much more. A virtual tour can be accessed on the school's website.

The students: The student population is 53.6% women and 46.4% men. While the majority are Pennsylvania residents, many come from nearby New York and New Jersey as well as 20 other states and four foreign nations.

Insight

Wilkes was founded to educate first-generation students. "What sets us apart from other colleges can't be measured by numbers on a page. Students succeed here because of the unique atmosphere and philosophy. At Wilkes you will find someone who believes in you," explains Mike Frantz, vice president of enrollment and marketing. "Our professors do everything they can to help students reach their goals. They even help them figure out what those goals are."

According to Frantz, Wilkes is actively looking for reasons to include B students. "We look for signs of potential," he says. "Our faculty and staff truly take a deep interest in students' dreams and aspirations." For those students struggling with any particular skills, Wilkes offers individual tutoring as well as a staff that assists in career strategies and study skills. "We can take any students if they honestly express the desire to improve," explains Frantz. "This campus is full of passionate faculty who treat students as equals and challenge them to strive towards greater accomplishments."

University of Wyoming

Laramie, WY

Address: Corner of Ninth and Ivinson, Laramie, WY 82071
Phone: 800-342-5996
Admissions email: why-wy@uwyo.edu
Website: www.uywo.edu

Admissions Stats

Percentage of applicants admitted: 94.8%
SAT range: 470-590 verbal, 490-600 math
ACT range: 20-26

Size

Number of undergraduates: 9,385

Costs

Tuition and fees: $2,721 in state, $7,545 out of state
Books and supplies: $1,000
On campus room and board and other expenses: $8,632
Off campus room and board and other expenses: $8,632

Academics

Favorite majors: business, management, marketing and related support services, social sciences, engineering, agriculture, agriculture operations and related sciences

The B Features

Academic Services provides support for undergraduates through tutoring and study skills development. It includes a series of study skills workshops and individual study skills advising.

Student Success Services are geared for students who meet one of these three criteria: first-generation college student, low-income family or documented disability. SSS offers individual and group tutoring, study skills workshops, individualized math assistance, career exploration and more to eligible students.

Xavier University Louisiana

New Orleans, LA

Address: One Drexel Drive, New Orleans, LA 70125-1098
Phone: 504-520-7388
Admissions email: apply@xula.edu
Website: www.xula.edu

Admissions Stats

Percentage of applicants admitted: 84.1%
SAT range: 440-550 verbal, 430-550 math
ACT range: 18-23 composite, 18-24 English, 17-23 math

Size

Number of undergraduates: 3,145

Costs

Tuition and fees: $11,300
Books and supplies: $1,000
On campus room and board and other expenses: $7,733
Off campus room and board and other expenses: $8,706

Academics

Favorite majors: psychology, business, management, marketing and related support services, biological and biomedical sciences, social sciences, physical sciences

---

The B Features

The Office of Academic Support Programs is where students go for that extra help they need in one-on-one tutoring, academic counseling, study techniques, test-taking strategies, reaching enrichment and development, time management skills and referrals to the math, reading and writing labs. Tutoring services are free.

The Math Lab helps student develop their mathematical abilities in an informal manner. The college states that the overall goal of the lab is to "increase each student's understanding of her or his course material. This takes time and active participation on the student's part."

Students may also use the Reading Lab to learn to read and study more effectively. Software can be utilized that helps improve vocabulary and comprehension skills. A Speech Lab is also available, as is a Writing Center website for online tutoring in the different stages of the writing process.

Index of America's Best Colleges for B Students

High Point University / 173
High Point, NC

Hiram College / 174
Hiram, OH

Hollins University / 175
Roanoke, VA

Hood College / 176
Frederick, MD

University of Houston / 177
Houston, TX

Howard University / 178
Washington, DC

University of Idaho / 179
Moscow, ID

Indiana State University / 180
Terre Haute, IN

Indiana University (Bloomington) / 181
Bloomington, IN

Indiana University of Pennsylvania / 183
Indiana, PA

University of Louisiana (Lafayette) / 184
Lafayette, LA

Lynn University / 186
Boca Raton, FL

McKendree College / 188
Lebanon, IL

University of Maine (Orono) / 190
Orono, ME

Marymount Manhattan College / 191
New York, NY

George Mason University / 192
Fairfax, VA

Manhattanville College / 193
Purchase, NY

Michigan State University / 194
East Lansing, MI

Mills College / 195
Oakland, CA

University of Mississippi / 196
University, MS

Mitchell College / 197
New London, CT

Montana Tech of the University of Montana / 199
Butte, MT

Morehouse College / 200
Atlanta, GA

University of Nevada-Las Vegas / 201
Las Vegas, NV

University of New Mexico / 202
Albuquerque, NM

University of New Orleans / 203
New Orleans, LA

University of North Carolina at Greensboro / 204
Greensboro, NC

Ohio University / 206
Athens, OH

Ohio Northern University / 208
Ada, OH

Ohio Wesleyan University / 210
Delaware, OH

Oregon State University / 211
Corvallis, OR

Pine Manor College / 213
Chestnut Hill, MA

Prescott College / 214
Prescott, AZ

SUNY College at Purchase / 216
Purchase, NY

Randolph-Macon College / 217
Ashland, VA

University of Redlands / 218
Redlands, CA

University of Rhode Island / 219
Kingston, RI

Rider University / 220
Lawrenceville, NJ

Rust College / 221
Holly Springs, MO

Saint John's University / 222
Collegeville, MN

Salve Regina University / 223
Newport, RI

University of San Francisco / 225
San Francisco, CA

Schreiner University / 226
Kerrville, TX

Shaw University / 228
Raleigh, NC

Simmons College / 229
Boston, MA

Sonoma State University / 230
Rohnert Park, CA

Spelman College / 231
Atlanta, GA

Suffolk University / 232
Boston, MA

Sweet Briar College / 234
Sweet Briar, VA

Temple University / 235
Philadelphia, PA

University of Tennessee / 236
Knoxville, TN

Thiel College / 237
Greenville, PA

Tuskegee University / 238
Tuskegee, AL

University of Utah / 239
Salt Lake City, UT

Washington State University / 240
Pullman, WA

Wells College / 241
Aurora, NY

Wesleyan College / 242
Macon, GA

Westminster College / 243
New Wilmington, PA

West Virginia University / 244
Morgantown, WV

Whittier College / 245
Whittier, CA

Wilkes University / 246
Wilkes-Barre, PA

University of Wyoming / 248
Laramie, WY

Xavier University Louisiana / 249
New Orleans, LA

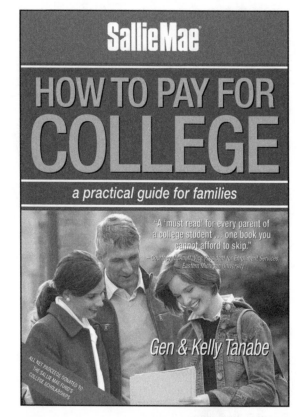

About the Author

Tamra Orr is a full time educational writer and author originally from Indiana and now living in the Pacific Northwest (where she takes a long look at the mountains every single day!) She is the author of more than 50 nonfiction titles for kids, teens and families. Her book, *Violence in Our Schools: Halls of Hope, Halls of Fear* (Scholastic, 2003), won the Best Nonfiction Book of the Year for Teens from the New York Public Library. She is also the author of *The Purple Cow Guide to Extraordinary Essays* (Scholastic, 2005) and *The Encyclopedia of Notable Hispanic-Americans* (Publications International, 2005).

Tamra is involved in education in almost every imaginable way. She writes dozens of nonfiction books each year on a huge variety of topics (from face lifts to fire ants!). She writes hundreds of stories and items for standardized tests for more than a dozen educational companies. She has a degree in Secondary Education and English from Ball State University in Muncie, Indiana. Tamra has been married for more than half of her life to Joseph and together, they have four children ranging in age from 21 to nine. The three that are still living at home are all homeschooled (in between her writing and his messing around with old Volkswagens). Tamra has appeared on numerous radio and television shows and has done countless book signings/appearances to promote her books and talk about a variety of issues within education. Since she was once so shy she almost flunked Speech in high school, this is still an amazing fact to her (and her parents!)

In addition to this book and other titles, Tamra is also the author of the forthcoming *Ace the SAT Writing Even If You Hate to Write: Shortcuts and Strategies to Score Higher Regardless of Your Skill Level* from SuperCollege (2006).

And to think she did all of this...and she was a mere B student!